KILL, BUBBA, KILL!

Bubba Smith and Hal DeWindt

A Ritter/Geller Book

A Wallaby Book
Published by Simon & Schuster, Inc.
New York

Copyright © 1983 by Ritter/Geller Communications

All rights reserved
including the right of reproduction
in whole or in part in any form
Published by Wallaby Books
A Division of Simon & Schuster, Inc.
Simon & Schuster Building
1230 Avenue of the Americas
New York, New York 10020

Designed by Leonard Telesca

WALLABY and colophon are registered trademarks of Simon & Schuster, Inc.

First Wallaby Books printing October 1983

10 9 8 7 6 5 4 3 2 1

Manufactured in the United States of America

ISBN: 0-671-47647-5

CONTENTS

Foreword by Hal DeWindt   7

Chapter **1**   The Whole Truth and Nothing But...   9

Chapter **2**   I Say I Was Born in Beaumont 'Cause I Couldn't Spell Nacogdoches   20

Chapter **3**   I Had to Be Twice As Good   32

Chapter **4**   Grab Everybody, Sort, Toss, 'Til I Find the One with the Ball—Keep Him!   51

Chapter **5**   I Had Watched *The Untouchables* on Television, So I Knew about Italians, But What the Hell Was a Jew?   70

Chapter **6**   Angel, Colt, and King   93

Chapter **7**   My Time   118

Chapter **8**   Revelations   155

Chapter **9**   ...The Truth, So Help Me...   168

Afterword   184

Dedicated to

My family
Stanley Cohen
Marty Blackman
John Murphy
Lew Ehrlich
Michigan State University
Pastor Frederick K. Price

Everyone who has accepted me as a person beyond football

Special thanks to

    Jack Artenstein
    Tony Cunningham
    Loretta Duerson
    Marti Freirich
    Deborah Gamble
    Bernadette Gradney
    Sid Holt
    Stan Hyman
    Gary and Pam Kleinman
    Ira Ritter
    Nils Shapiro
    Tom Shropshire
    City Council of Beaumont, Texas

                    —Bubba Smith

FOREWORD

"When hearing tales of Bubba Smith,
You wonder, is he man or myth?"
Ogden Nash

"The way people talk about him, you'd think he was the greatest thing since peanut butter."
Weeb Ewbank

This is the true story of an artist—an artist in a sport called football. This is the story of an Afro-American life that transcends sport and art. Bubba Smith was born February 28, 1945. That year Germany and Japan surrendered, Adolph Hitler committed suicide, and the atomic bomb exploded.

Charles Aaron Smith: six feet eight inches tall, two hundred seventy pounds; Texan, actor, and businessman. The son of Willie Ray, who, although crippled, has become the most successful high school football coach in Texas. The son of Georgia, a sublime lady who has earned a masters' degree in economics. The brother of two All-Americans and National Football League stars, Willie Ray, Jr., and Tody.

Bubba is all of the above—as well as a National Football

League first-round draft choice, twice All-American, Lineman of the Year, and as you will learn, a man who has undergone a sometimes unbelievably traumatic yet spiritual existence.

I have known him as a superstar since 1966—and as my best friend the past three years.

—Hal DeWindt

CHAPTER 1

The Whole Truth and Nothing But...

COACH SHULA SCREAMED, Don Shinnick led the prayer, and I—after a loss in the 1969 season—booked. In Black Texas *to book* meant *to leave*, but here I was in Baltimore, Maryland, surrounded by white.

Snow was falling, gliding down around my white Corvette, and white Memorial Stadium disappeared behind me as I drove down the white cemented streets toward home. The dulcet tones of Nat "King" Cole on the radio mellowed me, and the disappointing memory of my white-uniformed team faded from my mind. The final image was the white numbers on the scoreboard reading 20–13.

The fashionable, twenty-nine story building that I called home during the football season loomed before me. The white twin towers, one for singles and the other for married couples, grew more difficult to see as the snow fell more heavily. I turned left off Charles Street into the singles parking lot. Freshly scrubbed white tile surrounded my latest gift automobile as I followed the curves to my destination. I roared to my usual melodramatic stop, the tires screeching happily. I was home, I could relax.

Unfolding my frame as I stepped out of the sports car, I waved a silent goodbye to Nat Cole as I hummed the final bars of a Christmas song. Inside, the numbers above the elevator door flashed bright white as the machine rose to take me to my plush, white, furnished penthouse suite. The white doors motored open, and I ducked my Afroed head and climbed aboard the white-leathered elevator—you get used to avoiding doorframes when you're six eight with a five-inch Afro.

"You Bubba Smith?" he asked as the elevator doors eased shut. He was a white guy, lounging coolly at the back of the elevator, decked out in a spanking new herringbone sport coat and color-coordinated from his penny loafers to his velour sky hat. I nodded as we passed the second floor. Only the Muzak recording of "White Christmas" accompanied us.

He was the trip—a foot shorter than I, a hundred pounds lighter, and he didn't stretch his neck, like most people, when he talked to me. He looked squarely into my tinted glasses. "You know you stunk out the joint today!" I poked hard at the bridge of my shades and noticed for the first time that he had pressed the button marked 13. I squared my well-publicized shoulders and said, "Yeah?" That was my comeback to this pipsqueak, standing in my elevator, in my building, in my city.

We reached his floor, the doors opened and he glided out, saying "Later on, Bubba Smith!" The doors closed, I lit a Winston and blew out a smile. I liked his swaggering arrogance; he had a different kind of flair than I was used to. The midget had class. A Jewboy with style—now I've seen it all. I thought like that, then, before I got to know my best friend, Stanley.

The true odd couple: Stanley Cohen, 29, born and raised in Baltimore, Maryland, and Charles Aaron "Bubba" Smith, 24, from Beaumont, by way of Nacogdoches, Texas. An accomplished criminal lawyer and a quarterback crusher hanging tight and cool. His truthfulness had awakened me, reminding me of my past, of my father's honesty. My teammates had laid out that old rah-rah jive, and a midget stranger had popped me with how it really was. I knew we would see each other again. About people I'm always right on. About games people play, well man, that's another thing.

The next afternoon I found myself in the Playboy Club. On my menu was an unforgettable chestnut beauty named Dawn, a brand-new bunny on the afternoon shift. I could never understand how anyone could eat when she moved past their table—she was lusciously fine! There sat Stanley, my critic from the thirteenth floor, with Dawn bending over his right shoulder, taking his order. I waved my most professional hey-how-ya-doin' wave toward Stanley, hoping Dawn would take notice. She ignored me, and Stanley waved back casually. Suddenly Dawn's tray was in Stanley's lap. He didn't move, but stayed cool and looked at my beauty with complete disdain. She started to cry and ran into the kitchen. My chance was now. Smith to the rescue. I was great with the rescue routine.

I slid into the kitchen a few steps behind her, ready to soothe. I asked her if there was anything I could do to help—the Old Number 77 move from Michigan State. Dawn lifted her tearful, green eyes and stared blankly at me. Ah ha, I said to myself, step 1, check. She then denied me step 2, or any other, by saying, "I love that man more than my own life!" I waited for more, my admiration mounting steadily for this new dude that tells me off and takes my ladies. She finished by saying, "He just told me that he couldn't see me anymore!"

I came to the club to get a new lady and found myself respecting the competition. Damn, Stanley, lighten up, my man.

Every night Stanley and I were with the ladies, partying in my suite or his. The finest in America had to be on their toes for Blackman and Robin. We even made fun of the racial thing at a time when riots seemed to be breaking out every hour. Our sense of humor eased for us the tension that blazed hot during the '60s. If the country had dealt with the problem as he and I dealt with it, America would be what it was supposed to be.

Every other Sunday, we would rent a Silver Cloud Rolls Royce and drive to the stadium. Stanley would wear a chauffeur's cap and play his role to a bust. Instead of driving to where the players always parked on 33rd Street, we would drive straight up to the stadium's VIP entrance. Stanley would leap out, race to open the passenger door and bow respectfully. Stanley's lady, a fine white princess, would style out. I would follow, a full-length fur sweeping the ground as I dipped, whipped, and slipped into view. My lady, a bronze fox, would bring up the rear like a Hollywood starlet. The kids went crazy. "Do it up, Hubba Bubba!" "Get down, Bubba!" "My main man, Bub!" While signing autographs, I would motion to Stanley with my index finger. "Henry, make sure the ladies are properly seated." I always waited to give the order so that the wives of the other players would overhear and get unjointed. Stanley and the girls would grandly walk in through the gate toward their boxes as I bopped, bipped, and bumped to the players' entrance. Eat your heart out Sidney Poitier, Jim Brown, and Orange Juice.

We tried the old reverse move only once, when I drove Stanley and our companions to a plush country club, so plush that even Stanley was out of place. As we rolled to a stop, I leaped out and opened the door for the passengers. I tried the Stanley bow and felt my tight trousers split north, then south, in the crotch. That was bad enough, I thought, but it was carried further when one of the guests, hearing the *rrriiippp*, saw me and said, "That you, Bubba?" I could only crack up as I watched Stanley roll out of the door, screaming in laughter at my embarrassment.

We went on like Mutt and Jeff having an absolute ball. At the end of the 1971 season, Stanley leaped out of the bleachers after the Super Bowl game. He was very happy and very stoned as he celebrated our victory over Dallas. I caught him before he hit the ground. Our line coach, John Sandusky—the best coach and teacher, besides my father, I've ever had—tried to beat the fan off me. I explained to John that it was just crazy Cohen, the Counselor.

In 1972, three years after Stanley and I had met, was the time of trauma. I had requested a renegotiation of my contract—I had helped, as much as anyone, to win our first Baltimore Super Bowl. Carroll Rosenbloom, the owner of the Colts, refused. "Not policy!" he said. "Not policy, my ass!" was my response. We bounced it back and forth into the exhibition season and finally settled on a one-hundred-thousand-dollar furnished house.

When I reported, after everything was settled, to my first exhibition game, against the Pittsburgh Steelers, I was in top shape. It was the game that turned my life completely around.

It had rained for two hours in Tampa that July morning, yet by three o'clock the field was dry. Perhaps fatefully, Johnny Unitas said he had seen a snake by the bench. I wish I had acknowledged that sign that day in Florida.

In the first half, I sacked Terry Bradshaw five times. I enjoyed playing against the best professional athletes—it seemed I had all my greatest days against the finest competition. I was hot—it was 98 degrees—and the fans were screaming every time Bradshaw hit the grass, as they had at Michigan State in 1966. "Kill, Bubba, kill!" The fifth time Terry looked at me and shook his head, and I gave him my best hope-to-die-Colt look of defiance. I was a team man to my jockstrap.

Coach McCafferty, in his second year after winning the Super Bowl his first, made his usual way-to-work speech to the team. Mac found me at my locker where I was sneaking my supply of Winston cigarettes for the meeting of the defense. He patted me on the butt and gave me my own way to go. The team had lost their first two exhibition games, and Mac wanted this game bad.

I sat out the third quarter, but the dynasty that was to supplant the Colts, the Steeler offense, started cooking. They were getting closer and closer. I saw John Sandusky look my way, and I began stretching my happy-to-go-back-but-what-am-I-going-back-in-for body. The six feet eight inches and two hundred eighty pounds of Beaumont Beef bounced back. I jogged on the field using my Tody Smith stride. The Tody stride is a composite of a hungry panther stalking and Fred Astaire striding. It seemed to work—the crowd welcomed me.

The very first play saw quick Rick Volk intercept a Bradshaw pass. I had rushed the quarterback and had forced an early release thrown too early. For the first time in my life I peeled back to block on an interception. I moved over to block Harris and ended up aiming for Ron Shanklin. I threw my body at Ron and missed him, but I hit a line marker with such force that it drove the pole into the ground. Fifty-eight thousand people who had moments before cheered my flamboyance were stone silent. It was my time. All I could do was scream. Three torn ligaments, one crushed cartilage, a ripped tendon, and one ambulance later, I was in the emergency room talking long distance to my mother. I cried. "I'm sorry. I let you down. I ran into the marker; the fool holding it forgot to let go!" Mother as usual sobered me and made me feel loved. "Sweetheart, you've never let Mama down!"

I was flown home to Baltimore's Memorial Hospital at 5:00 AM. They operated for four hours, drilling through the kneecap. A very complicated but successful operation, they told me as I came out from under the anesthesia. I fell asleep dreaming about my glory days, that Super Bowl dream—I heard the crowd . . . I saw the field . . . I saw the bodies fall . . . I heard the grunts . . . I began to laugh—waking up to pure pain. The drugs began; the fire dissolved; my life was over, I thought.

My eyes awoke to the dawning sun. The golden circle surrounded my mother's beautiful smiling face. My father, the

Coach, was looking dapper. He winked hello to me. The talk and laughter came in waves. The tears remained constant. So did the drugs.

"Peeped your performance on the tube, Cuddy Cuddy. Damn, you're clumsy!" It was the weird one, Stan "the Man" Cohen. "I would have been here earlier, but I had to file the lawsuit." "Who you suing now, Counselor?" My voice sounded as if I was talking through gauze. "Me? You, Smith. You're suing the NFL for negligence!" "Sheeet," I said, forgetting Mother. "Your son has a filthy mouth, Reta Baby!" Mother covered her mouth and giggled. I felt myself laugh. "Do we have a chance?" I asked Stanley. "Eighty thousand to one, Bubba, eighty thousand to one. We might make history, Negro person," the Counselor continued, "you and Martin Luther King." He paused to see if his audience was still awake. I looked at my buddy and said, "Let's go!"

I always had great comebacks for Stanley. A few years earlier it had been "Yeah!" Now it was "Let's go!" The main ingredient, though, was that we fought them together, Cohen and Smith, or better still, Smith and Cohen. It had a certain ring. I'll tell you more about the hospital later; now it's about truth.

Six years later in 1978, we added another lawyer, Tony Cunningham. Cohen couldn't take a civil case, so he asked me to check out a friend of his and see if I liked him. An hour after meeting Tony Cunningham, I knew we would win. Besides having the look of a winner and creative ideas about how he would defeat the National Football League, he was a Scorpio. I was into astrology in those days, and I knew two Scorpios who were definite killers, my former wife and Jack Tatum, a teammate on the Raiders. And I certainly needed a killer on my side.

Howard Cosell, Don Meredith, Curly Culp, and Dr. Robert Rosenfeld, among many, had taken the time to testify on my behalf. It seemed to be going along better than I had expected. The trial was in its third week and I was suing one of the largest corporations in America, the National Football League, and it began to look like we had a chance. Tony Cunningham had stopped biting his nails, and Stanley Cohen, who sat behind me every day, began grinning.

Then it came. Like being hit from the blind side in a game.

The league had called Miami's former coach, George Wilson, as an expert on reading game films. Wilson testified that a Steeler's block had caused my injury. We had maintained that a line marker held by a NFL employee had destroyed my knee and my glory years. The jury didn't know who to believe. So, we were forced to find him.

It had never entered my mind—a block! He was not part of the play. True, we were playing the Pittsburgh Steelers that night in 1972. True, he was the rookie sensation of the year. True, he was on the field in Tampa Stadium at that very moment, yet so were twenty-one other players, and he was chosen. "Why?" Stanley asked. I couldn't answer.

Tony went back to biting his nails. I returned to wondering what would be next. Our hand had been called. Two and a half million dollars were at stake. What did I expect Pete Rozelle and his half dozen lawyers to do, roll over? There were a hundred other guys waiting in the wings with lawsuits in hand.

I had the ball on their five-yard line before Wilson's testimony. The game had suddenly turned around. I didn't mind that. In fact, being an athlete since I was a kid meant I was used to change. My problem was the sneak play—imagine a team putting a second ball in the game with a twelfth man. We were after the twelfth man. All is fair in love and war.

It was war! Twenty-four telephone calls later, Stanley had him on the phone. He was relaxing after a hard day of filming a television program in Jamaica. I took the phone and told him what had been said, what Wilson had testified. There was silence on the other end. He said that he had heard that the trial had begun but nothing more. The National Football League had smothered any news coming out of the trial, an impressive show of power. No one knew what was happening. I did my best to fill him in. I even remember adding a few lightweight jokes to relax the tension. Another long long pause. He would come. He would set the story straight. He was fired up, and so was I. I thanked him, hung up, and thanked God. I believe I spent most of another sleepless night thanking God, Jesus Christ, my father, my mother, Stanley, and Tony. I was into a thank thing that day in 1978.

He had to go home to Pittsburgh first. So the Learjet I rented flew from Jamaica to Pittsburgh and finally to Tampa. This city had seen my blood spill out six years before and now watched as my money poured out, a quarter of a million dollars of it, but it was worth it, I kept repeating to myself. Anyone who knows me knows how careful I am with money. Mother would have had a migraine if she had known how much I was spending. I was telling the truth, though, the way she had taught me.

I had not known Franco Harris as a man, but I was positive that he was one of the few. When you have lived a sport all of your natural life; when your father is one of the great football coaches of all time; when both of your brothers are All-Americans, two of the best to play the game; you understand the word *professional*. Franco had proven his worth on the field, and now it was his turn to prove it off. He had come a long way since that night in 1972. He was second to the all-time great Jim Brown in rushing. I welcomed him, as a professional, when he arrived that muggy night at the Tampa airport.

The next morning was all business. I felt like I was playing ball again. The adrenaline was flowing. I was ready. We viewed the film of the 1972 exhibition game. My nerves were irritated by a minor projector problem, but Stanley was calm enough to repair it. I had not noticed in the film before that Franco was in the area. There he was, number 32. I was running at top speed, however, a good yard in front of him. I had seen the film a hundred times or more, so many viewings that the big guy in the Colts uniform, me, number 78, was just another body. Just another body until I hit the marker. It returned then, the echo of the pain. Tony switched on the lights as my hands had reflexively moved to protect my right knee. My eyes were on Franco.

"I never touched him! I never touched him!" Franco said it. I heard it! Stanley grinned. "I never touched him," I repeated. I'll never forget those four humongous words. Replaying them in my head, they began to sound better than Aretha's "Respect," Ray Charles's "Georgia," and Stevie's "Visions in My Mind." Well, the vision in my mind at that very moment was—touchdown. Stanley and Tony shook hands, and I blessed Franco.

Olympic champion John Carlos would have been proud as both my clenched fists shot up victoriously. Tony had to ask him, "Would you say that on the witness stand?" Franco looked at me curiously with his furrowed brow, a look that said, Why ask me that? Then he said, casually, "Of course."

I tried to play it off, but my long legs stumbled as I rose from the couch. I shook his hand and looked him squarely in the eyes, and he changed the subject to his long jet flight. The only thing I could come up with to say was "Yeah." I do that a lot.

Yeah! We walked toward the courthouse, the sun shining, at least for me. Franco and I appeared as huge bookends for the five-foot nine-inch Stanley and the even shorter Tony. Cunningham had a new spring in his gait since hearing Franco's news. I smiled at my lawyer and smelled the perfumed smoke pouring out of his brain, those brilliant wheels churning in that head of his.

Franco had a lazy rolling stroll. I strode as I did when we'd won the Super Bowl against Dallas in Miami in 1971. Tony and Stanley skipped to keep up.

Stanley left us at the steps of the courthouse, telling us that he'd join us later. He had to tell his mother the good news. With my head held high, my father's son, the team continued onward and upward. A six-foot Robert Redford–looking cat stood by one of the colonial pillars holding up the courthouse. He introduced himself as Pete Rozelle's lawyer. His manner was professionally friendly, and his eyes were clear and innocent. He asked Franco if he could talk with him for a few minutes, and Franco nodded yes and shook his hand. Tony and I continued on to courtroom 3. Tony looked at me. I poked at my glasses, smiled, and patted him on the back. "Nothing to worry about, my man." I meant it. Franco Harris in one minute had become my brother—brother superstar, brother truth, and brother black. My brother was with me in my troubling hour. No problem, Tony understood. Twenty-five minutes later Stanley slipped into his seat. Tony whispered the Rozelle lawyer news to Stanley at his arrival, and he played it off.

Brother Harris was called to the witness stand after the gavel and the hear-ye-hear-ye's had awakened the court. The undistinguished-looking judge leaned back in his fat, leather chair, folded his fat arms, and watched Franco walk toward him with the same fluid cool that flowed through the best defensive lines in football. He was sworn in by a stammering bailiff as Franco called out his name proudly, his hand wearing a Super Bowl ring placed firmly on the Bible. The legend of modern-day football sat down and smiled the famous Harris smile and appeared tired but relaxed.

Tony popped out of his chair like a gazelle. For the first time that day I noticed that Cunningham was wearing his poor-folks suit. Stanley told me once, months before the trial, about Tony's wardrobe for the jury. He'd dress to make the jury, mostly average citizens, relate to him. Tony was on it. I rose up in my chair awaiting the magic and the applause of victory. I winked at Stanley, who returned a fist salute, then poked at my glasses and smiled my secret smile.

He reached the witness chair and I could see that Tony was

positive that Franco's looks had locked the female vote on the jury. The males, even the crackers, liked a black football hero—we were looking good. I found myself rooting for him like a fan. My father, Willie Ray, Sr., had told me about Joe Louis, the heavyweight champion of the world, who raised millions of dollars during World War II for the American war machine and had said, "We gonna win this war because we on God's side." This was World War III for me, and I prayed that Franco looked enough like Joe to be as effective.

Thereupon, Franco Harris, being first duly sworn to tell the truth, the whole truth, and nothing but the truth, was examined and testified as follows.

DIRECT EXAMINATION

BY MR. CUNNINGHAM:

> THE CLERK: State your name.
> THE WITNESS: Franco Harris
> THE CLERK: Spell your last name for the record.
> THE WITNESS: H-a-r-r-i-s.

BY MR. CUNNINGHAM:

> Q. Mr. Harris, would you tell us what your occupation is, sir?
> A. Professional football player.
> Q. How long have you been doing that, Mr. Harris?
> A. Just finished six years.
> Q. What is your position generally that you play, sir?
> A. Running back.
> Q. And for what team do you play presently in professional football?
> A. I play for the Pittsburgh Steelers.
> Q. Have you always played for them during your professional career, sir?
> A. Yes, I have.
> Q. In 1972, Mr. Harris, were you involved in a professional football game here in Tampa, Florida?
> A. Yes, I was.
> Q. What position were you playing? In the same one?
> A. Running back, yes. . . .
> Q. Mr. Harris, I believe I asked you and you have testified

that you examined the film which is Plaintiff's Exhibit 3 and 4, which were reviewed on the projector?
A. Yes, I did examine them. . . .
Q. Did you review that film to your satisfaction to as best you could refresh your recollection concerning that game?
A. As best I could, yes.
Q. All right, sir. And in that particular game, one particular play is shown, is that correct?
A. Yes.
Q. Mr. Harris, do you personally remember, regardless of the film, do you personally remember anything about that particular play?
A. Okay. Before?
Q. Just yes or no.
A. Before seeing the film?
Q. Before seeing the film.
A. No, I didn't remember.

I played it back in my head. "No, I didn't remember!" The same voice, the same face, the same brother who had said, just hours before "I never touched him!" Why? I asked myself. A quality athlete had punked out. A brilliant star had fallen into the mud. I was humiliated for him. I ached inside and cried silently for him. I couldn't look at either Stanley or Tony.

I poked at my glasses, slid down into my chair, and tripped the journey of escape into a pattern of memories I had hoped to forget. Franco Harris couldn't remember and, oh my God, I could. I could see the painful pictures. They flickered like an old-fashioned movie. My ex-wife; drugs; Joe Thomas, the Baltimore Colts' general manager; the veterans of the Colts in my rookie year; coach Bum Phillips in my final year in the NFL; Duffy, my coach at Michigan State; George Egland in high school; and last but most vividly, my idol, my brother Beaver.

CHAPTER 2

I Say I Was Born in Beaumont 'Cause I Couldn't Spell Nacogdoches

ON A DRY SPRING DAY in 1934, the infamous Bonnie and Clyde crossed paths with the Smiths from Denton, Texas.

The New York Times, May 24, 1934: Gabe Wright, a Negro, captured J. B. French, a lifer, one of the four who escaped with Hamilton, when French entered his cabin the next day. All the others, including Ray Hamilton, were picked up, one by one, but not before they had done further damage. . . . At Grapevine, Texas, on the morning of April 2, 1934, State Highway Patrolmen F. B. Wheeler and H. D. Murphy were passing a car parked in the road when, without warning, machine guns mowed them down. Clyde Barrow's fingerprints were found on a whiskey bottle at the spot.

Clyde Barrow was heard from again when Hamilton went on trial in Texas following his capture in Sherman, Texas. He sent a mocking letter to the authorities in which he scoffed at Hamilton for a published statement that he was the instigator of all the killings. Hamilton was sentenced to 362 years in prison.

The mocking letter included a threat that Bonnie and Clyde would come to pay a visit to the jail where Hamilton was caged.

The jailhouse was in Denton, Texas, the birthplace of Willie Ray Smith, Bubba's father.

"The chickenshit police were shakin' in their little booties!" recalls Mitchell "Foots" Jackson, cousin of Willie Ray. "They all jumped in their little cars and scrammed to the wrong damn highway on purpose. Bonnie and Clyde told everyone their route and time of arrival." A gleam shows in Mitchell's eye. "It was forty-eight years ago, but I can remember everything like it was yesterday. Yes I can. I scooted my little twelve-year-old behind over to the town square with the rest of the guys. We didn't have to wait too long, ol' Clyde was right on time. If nothing else, white folks were on time. Clyde had written that they were comin' between 2:15 and 2:30 PM in his letter, and here they came in that gray Ford car." Mitchell is rolling with the memory.

"A small black-headed man, a smaller red-haired gal, and a big ol' brown machine gun. We all scattered when they let loose on that old gun. All kinds of bullet holes were in the jailhouse, and they kept on truckin'. Yes, they did! But that ain't the best part! Willie Ray's twin sister, Ida May, got a better look at Bonnie and Clyde than we did!" Mitchell says, smiling.

"I shouldn't laugh. Excuse me. It wasn't funny at all then. We got the word from Woody Simms. Fat, greasy Woody came running back and told us. Bonnie and Clyde had decided to get some spending money from the gas station at the edge of town. 'They busted in,' said Woody, 'tied up pretty Ida May with chicken wire, snatched the cash, and took off in that Ford. Bonnie and Clyde were laughing their natural brains out and Ida May Smith was thoroughly pissed." Mitchell tries to stop his laughter. "I really don't mean to bust up like this, but I can see Ida May when they walked in. She kept tellin' everyone that she told Bonnie and Clyde to stop being bad people. No wonder they were laughing as they tied her up. Ida May still got the scar on the side of her mouth to prove it.

"They were lucky Doll wasn't there. [Doll was Willie Ray's first nickname.] He'd've probably started telling Bonnie and Clyde those stories about the ghosts down by the graveyard or gotten them involved in some sports stories about famous Negroes. Ol' Doll—he was about 22—stayed decked out and was always as clean as a mosquito's peter. Yes, he was! He was our hero! White folks killed each other while Doll taught us everything we needed to know from sports to sportin'."

Mitchell's remembered pride in his friend and teacher shows in his eyes.

"All the kids in Denton made Doll our teacher—he could do no wrong. We were the group who would celebrate life four, maybe five, times a week down at the Place with a midnight dinner, as Doll named it. Midnight dinners were a five-cent peanut patty, and if you were really sticken with cash, a five-cent slice of watermelon. Radio station KDNT would be jumpin' with race records. The place was down a little ways, from Prairie Street, near where the trucks used to stop. Peetie Wheatstraw, the Devil's Son-in-Law, the High Sheriff of Hell, would bleed the blues. Art Tatum would be working on some "Wee Baby Blues" and Duke, Cab, and Chick Webb all supplied the background sounds for our midnight dinners!

"Doll passed down his experiences to us and probably saved our lives with his wisdom." He was one of seven children sternly raised by Hattie Alberta Smith, a six-foot African-Indian who had little assistance from her absentee husband, Walter. "And from what I saw, she didn't need any."

Willie Ray "Doll" Smith interrupts. "We dreamed about the Place . . . our place. Although it wasn't anything fancy, it was like a haven to us. A yellow-painted wooden-and-aluminum shack, sometimes called a cafe, was special because of all the love that took place among us. You've got to remember these were hard segregation years and we bronzed Americans weren't allowed everywhere in the country we loved.

"We Negroes were different from other Americans in many ways, especially on June 19, 1934. Every year on this day in our great, big Lone Star State of Texas, Negroes took a holiday, a break from the routine for twenty-four too-fast hours. It was our Independence Day—the news of the end of the Civil War reached Texas two months late—and this day is called Juneteenth. Don't laugh now—it could have had a lot worse name.

"Huge deep holes were dug in the ground of Denton. We used everything we could lay our hands on, from a shovel for the hinkty Negroes to our bare hands for us. That was on the seventeenth of June," Willie Ray remembers. "You had to stretch wire across the openings to secure the pits. The slabs of meat were barbequed on the eighteenth, and on the nineteenth all Heaven broke loose as we partied our black, brown, and beige behinds off.

"All day long, ball games, dances, eatin', drinkin', and of

course bones. Everyone was celebrating, except for a few angry young men who had other fish to fry. A fight broke out that year down by the south side of the Church of God in Christ. The heat of the day was beginning to ease, but John Reilly's temper was rising by the second. John had squared off opposite his own blood brother, little Wesley. The crime—messin' with his gal. When I reached the church, I could see John's eyes blazing with jealous pain. Mr. Reilly's was as serious as a black heart attack. Standing around the two brothers were of course the signifiers. Signifying is an art in Texas, and most street people do it with gusto. What they were doing was provoking John's anger more and more. Sanford Williams, Raymond Bowers, Rufus Smith, Mitch, and a lot of nameless faces were playfully provoking the problem. Their taunts were making me angry," "so I could imagine what they were doing to John. Suddenly out pops this shotgun. Where it came from, I can't tell to this day. But John was holding it dead at his brother's throat. As soon as I saw the gun, I also spied Sanford Williams edging closer and closer. In one electrifying moment it all happened. I heard the report from the gun. It was like a backfire car, a huge camara flash, and a thousand bees buzzing in my thigh bone."

Independence Day, Juneteenth 1934, had become Willie Ray Smith's time. Eighteen wasted months in the St. Paul Hospital in Dallas, and the deep wound refused to heal.

"The doctors gave me thirty days to live on this earth if I wanted to keep my leg. Mama came visiting me and asked, 'What ya going to do, Willie Ray?' 'I'm going to live thirty days! I came in with my leg, I'll leave with my leg!' I decided.

"I was lying there all depressed and all of a sudden the door swung open and in walked a talented, fresh lookin' doctor. I knew what he was going to say before he opened his no-lip mouth. 'We gonna try something brand new, boy,' he said. His name was Doctor Samuels and he was glowing like an angel. 'I was expecting you!' I said, smiling my best smile."

The next morning Smitty awakened with a screen wire over the wound, and a portable light fixed above the wire. "I got out of that bed to wash my hands and peeped down at the wire contraption. I almost blacked out. God help me! You know how it is when you feel like somebody's dimmed the damn lights all of a sudden? Well, that's what happened to ol' Smitty. I staggered back to the bed and rang for the nurse. She came in like a bowl of jello, with that cornpone look on her silly but angelic face. All I could do was point down at hundreds of tiny white maggots eating away my flesh," Smitty quietly concludes.

"I never did anything without a flourish or two. Never gave up even when it could have been justified by the average man. I was 'crippled for the rest of my life,' but the experience seems to have strengthened my spirit," says Willie Ray Smith.

Three hundred miles down the road a piece, as is everything in Texas, a charming chestnut-colored young lady was preparing to leave the town of Nacogdoches. Miss Lady's name was Georgia Oreatha Curl, and she was sixteen years old.

A 30-degree chill was in the air, and tinsel-topped Christmas trees rested near garbage cans, exhausted from their week of labor on Harvard Street. The smell of freshly chopped wood burning filled the air. And here she was, bright eyed and bushy tailed, our Georgia leaving for college. She had chopped cotton, cooked, cleaned and scrubbed, walked six miles to her one-dollar-and-fifty-cents-a-week job as a maid for Mrs. Mishot on Baker Street, went to church every Sunday, and had been a very good little girl, except when she tore up on a few little girls who had sorry mouths. Now Georgia Curl was on her way to Prairie View College, and she was ready for anything but what was to come.

In 1936 the good ol' Red, White, and Blue was fighting its war against the Great Depression; the Swastika was warming up for war in Europe; the Rising Sun was at war in Asia, and our Lone Star miss was thinking of everything else but. Miss Georgia was focused on her future. Her reign of charm had ended at Nacogdoches Colored High School (official name). Watch out, Prairie View, here she comes! Here comes Doodlebug—that was her nickname.

She bade farewell to her classmates, sisters, starring roles in local plays, the undefeated basketball team, a favorite teacher named Lillian Griffin, and a puppy love affair with Buford Powell. Mother Lonie Curl, of Irish-Indian extraction, concealed her emotions by saying, "Business is business; play is play. Put everything you have into everything you do." Mama Curl had put everything she had into the switch too many times on other instructional occasions, thought lovely Georgia, but she smiled graciously—and left. A rough six-hour train trip in the colored car carried Georgia into the unknown.

While Georgia listened to the train whistle its way toward Houston and Prairie View, back in Denton, Willie Ray Smith could only think of Wilma Delores Bell. He was crushed after being turned down by her. She lived with her family across the street, and they had had a thing going before his accident. Now the thing had left, and Willie was thinking seriously of going left of life—suicide was on his mind, for a minute. Bonnie and Clyde's pal, Ida May, saved her twin brother by stopping him from taking an overdose of pills. It was Wilma's parents who had told Willie to forget it after they saw he was a cripple. Papa Bell was thoroughly insistent, and Wilma obeyed him and his shotgun.

It was impossible for Willie to stay in Denton, a town that had broken his heart and body. He decided to return to school after relearning something he had never believed but had always known: many people judge others by the man on the outside, not the man on the inside, and never by his heart. He asked his mother for a little financial help and received more from the state department of rehabilitation. A graduate of Booker T. Washington High School in Dallas, he needed a college degree to obtain new respectability. His choice of school was of course fated by the love he and Georgia never imagined they would find. They both came to Prairie View.

The site of their first meeting wasn't particularly sublime—but the moment they saw each other they were both taken. The second meeting—now this is more romantic—was at the get-acquainted dance for freshmen.

Willie Ray Smith was resplendent in one of his fifty-two suits, the shadow blue. As he stood at the top of the stairs, those eyes searched the room for his young lady. There she was, in delicate red, glowing with happiness. How can this crippled man dance? was the only question in her mind.

Mitchell and the other disciples of the Doll of Denton would have been proud of their instructor, yes, they would. Not only did Willie Ray dance with Georgia, he swept her into a new world, and he sang. The orchestra played "Music, Maestro, Please," and Willie Ray Smith, former member of the Ambassador's, a singing group at his high school, crooned his huge heart out as he glided Doodlebug across, around, and beyond the dance floor.

That evening Doodlebug became Reta Baby, from her middle name, Oreatha, and a beautiful woman. She had never entertained love in her detailed, coordinated plans. If she had, it wouldn't have included a cripple; but like Willie Ray, Georgia understood that this man was not disabled in any sense of the word. She had met disabled men all of her life, all of them with well-formed limbs but no heart.

They knew it then; yet she was seventeen, and he was twenty-five. Georgia needed time.

In the sophomore year, 1937, a slight problem in communication arose. "I had gotten so involved with Georgia that when my mother telephoned from Denton to ask if I'd be home for Christmas, I said, 'No, ma'am, I'm not coming home; I'm staying on campus with my gal!'" Willie Ray says proudly. "'But please send me a box of food!' Mother agreed to send the food, and I was ready for Santa Claus and all the trimmings. I remembered, after the fact, that I hadn't asked Georgia about her plans. I dropped by that freezing afternoon and eased into the subject. Reta Baby just smiled and said, 'Oh, I *must* go home to Nacogdoches!' Two days later the food came, and Reta Baby had gone. I was left alone with a box of cold food in a cold dormitory, in December in Prairie View," sulks Willie Ray.

"I waited for her to return, and when the train pulled in, I saw her get off with a young punk. I couldn't take it! I saw a pretty student who had been in one of my classes and was crazy about me. I called her over and asked her to help me. She agreed, and arm in arm we walked up to Georgia and her friend. Her name was Mary Emma Graves, and she was stacked like a brick shithouse. I knew Mary would make an impression on Reta Baby." A gleam of delight fills Willie Ray's eyes.

WILLIE RAY: Hi!
GEORGIA: Oh hi! This is my home boy, Buford Powell.
WILLIE RAY: Buford?
GEORGIA: Yes, Buford.
WILLIE RAY: How do you do, Buford. This is my girlfriend, Miss Graves.
GEORGIA: It's nice to meet you, Miss *Waves*.
WILLIE RAY: That was Graves. The lady's name is Graves!
GEORGIA: Oh, I'm sorry. You two have a good time now, you hear. I'll see you on campus tomorrow, Willie Ray Smith!

"She turned on her heel, with Buford in tow, and fumed away. Glorious Graves and I left walking, but once we were out of their sight, we began jogging and laughing. It was a funny situation, or was it? Here I was acting like a kid—what was wrong with me? Or what was right with me? And who was that punk named Buford?"

They made up the next day, both finally confessing their love for each other. More games were played: the question of why Willie Ray's hands were softer than Georgia's came up. The answer came as Willie Ray attempted to prove his ability to work, so much so that he fainted. Willie Ray was not cut out for menial tasks, and he earned a new nickname, Sweetheart.

The pair worked hard at their studies, and both hustled to pay for their tuition, their books, and other expenses. Time passed by the lovers so quickly that when their graduation came, they were thrilled and almost surprised that they had fulfilled the college's requirements and, more important, their own.

There were no teaching jobs available. Georgia went to Freeport, Texas, and worked as a maid for an affluent family and taught classes to adults two nights a week. Not letting her too far out of sight, Willie Ray secured a job at Stauffer Chemical Company, half a mile away.

Angleton, Texas, is down the road a piece from Houston. It was made famous on July 18, 1940. There is a barbershop near the outskirts of this small town with one of those peppermint revolving signs hanging outside and sawdust carpeting the floor and a huge, round mirror hanging inside, which reflected love that memorable day. Georgia Oreatha Curl became Mrs. Willie Ray Smith, and Doll had caught his Doodlebug.

Mr. and Mrs. Smith honeymooned in their home—servants' quarters in Freeport.

There was an Axis raid at dawn on Cairo; German planes bombed Birmingham; the British bombed the Rhineland; and General MacArthur reported from Australia that in a Japanese air raid on Darwin, nine of the enemy planes were shot down with the loss of only one American plane. Negroes were rioting in Detroit, and Reta Baby was having one. A baby that is, the first for the Smiths of Freeport.

It was spring 1942. Love was in the air; the world had gone berserk; and all was well with the Smiths. There was a problem, but it was only money. The saying "Not poor, just broke" fitted the Smiths to a tee. Together their wages added up to twenty-six dollars and fifty cents. Not having to pay rent while living in the servants' quarters of Georgia's employers helped ends meet. Their Prairie View educations saved the day. Reta Baby even found a way to put a down payment on a desperately needed 1939 Ford, for a trip was imperative. Nacogdoches was about to experience sudden population growth: Georgia was to live with her mother until the birth of her child, while Willie Ray hung on in Freeport and saved the cash.

The Smiths planned, brilliantly, but after stage 1 had been achieved—Georgia in Nacogdoches—someone should have called the weather bureau. One month after she left, Hurricane Deborah came roaring through Freeport and ripped it clean apart.

Georgia pushed the curtains aside to see who could be knocking at the door at 3:00 AM, afraid that the knocking would wake her mother. She saw her husband standing drenched in the doorway. Willie Ray had driven two hundred miles in the rain, with everything that he could salvage in the back of their car.

"You won't believe what happened!" Willie held her face and looked deeply into Georgia's eyes. "They let me in the front door of Abner's Restaurant this afternoon. So much rain, I guess they couldn't see my color." They held onto each other tight that night.

The next evening brought good news as Willie Ray shouted from the street, "Reta Baby, Reta Baby, guess what? I got a job coaching and teaching science at Dunbar High School in Lufkin!" Georgia couldn't believe it, and she fell into her seat. Mama Lonie rushed to her to find out if she was all right. "I'm fine, Mama, just fine. I'm a little surprised, aren't you?" She directed the question at her husband. "At what, baby?" smiled Willie Ray. "At what? I can understand your teaching science, but when did you get this education in coaching? Coaching what?" asked Georgia. "Football and basketball!" replied Willie Ray. "What do you know about football and basketball? And how can you coach sports in your condition?" "I'm in great shape!" laughed Willie Ray. "Did they notice your leg?" asked Mama Lonie. "All the males are in the service. Coach Franklin was inducted into the army last week! I'm the most eligible man for the job. Uncle Sam don't want me!"

The syrupy charm of Sweetheart had helped him slither past the hard-nosed attitude of Frank Thomas, the principal of Dunbar, but could he summon the ol' Midnight Supper magic that had worked so well on the men of Denton? This was another time, another place. This and many other questions passed through the mind of the new coach as he limped toward the twenty strong-looking youngsters who were gathered in groups, watching him skeptically. Coach Smith played it off, though, and put on a performance that would have made Knute Rockne, Vince Lombardi, and Richard Pryor proud.

"He just stared through us for a minute or two," remembers Dr. Ronald Webb, one of Dunbar High School's questioning twenty. "We came to attention—it was almost automatic." Coach Smith, using his best baritone began, "Boys, I'm your new coach, but in honesty, I'm not your coach." They looked at each other, these innocent boys, who were pretending to be men. "Your coach is still coach Franklin who has been inducted into your country's armed forces. Each and every one of you will be playing for him, not me. He deserves your work. He deserves your concentration. You will use the same plays that he has taught you, and I will always be standing by to guide you however I can." He paused to let his remarks sink in. He turned and limped away, shouting over his shoulder, "Don't let coach Franklin down!" It seemed to work. The team's attitude was serious, and they listened, but coach Smith couldn't depend on one rah-rah speech to do the job. He began a cram course with a veteran coach, A. T. Miller of Wichita Falls. Miller worked Willie Ray's behind off until he learned the sport of football. He advised him to experiment with new ideas—"It's the only way to win"—and Willie knew he was right.

Lots of hours and no pay. The take home was fifty-nine dollars a month. The Smith's made do because they were smart people with faith in their future.

He made mistakes, one his wife remembers with glee. "He yelled at one of his tackles one day at practice," she laughs. "Fat Stuff Sewell," the Coach screamed, "all right, Sewell, get in your position!" Sewell replied humbly, "I am, I am in my tackle position." "Well, act like a tackle," the Coach shouted back without blinking an eye. He didn't know one position from another.

Most of the youngsters gravitated toward one player, Oscar Kennedy, and the Coach named him the team captain. He told Kennedy the truth. "I am not familiar with any of the plays in the game, but I can guide all of you as an objective viewer and a best friend." Oscar was sold, but he had one question. "What happened to your leg, Coach?" After he was told, his eyes grew round as saucers, his mouth hung open, and he hurried away toward his teammates to tell them the story.

The first game was won against a superior Jacksonville Negro High School team. The Dunbar team spirit, they said, was overwhelming. The second game was played on the road. The team bus was a cattle truck. "There is something about young Negroes. Despite all the pressure, they are still motivated by their hearts. When you think that these boys were asked to ride in a truck that only yesterday housed cattle—I knew then that my being there, working with these people, meant more than money. I had to be strong!" says Willie Ray proudly.

Coach Smith was away, traveling with his boys of Dunbar High, when on October 7, 1942, Oreatha Ray was born to Georgia Oreatha Smith in her mother's house on Harvard Street. "Her skin was like velvet, and her eyes were emeralds!" says Georgia. Problems occurred, however, problems that could not be anticipated by Doctor Robert Hansen, an Afro-American, a Negro in 1942. His brother was fighting in Europe against the Nazis, and he was home tending to his people, his American people. Robert Hansen was a doctor who was not allowed to use the hospital facilities of Nacogdoches.

Oreatha Ray Smith died three days after birth. "She never cried until she was dying," mumbles Georgia. Coach Smith never saw his daughter alive. In that year seventy-three out of every one thousand Negro infants died before age 1.

Life comes from the inside, and so did the light that shone through the eyes of the Doll, a light accompanied by his infectious smile, a dozen roses, and his beige 1942 threads. "Reta Baby, don't you worry none. We'll have another child soon, and it'll be a boy!"

Winner is a winner is a winner, and Coach Smith was surely a winner. Hadn't he managed, in his first year at Lufkin, to win nine football games out of ten and achieve a .500 percent record in basketball without knowing either sport? The spirit of the Smith's was never just talk. Three months after the death of her first child Georgia announced that she was pregnant again.

The I Formation was invented by coach Smith in 1943. Of the twenty-nine young men who reported to practice that summer, only sixteen made the team. Only the best survived in this small town of ten thousand people; the other nine thousand were in the stands cheering Dunbar High School to its first district championship—and the team now traveled by bus, not a cattle truck. Coach Willie Ray Smith had become a Texas success.

The good Doctor Hansen did his job on October 15, 1943, despite his not being allowed to use the hospital again. He delivered the first Smith baby to survive the ignorance of the country that they loved. The child was a boy and his name of course was Willie Ray, Jr. His father drove his Dunbar squad to eleven victories in its 1944 twelve-game season. The coach was on a roll; the team was on a roll, and Georgia was on her way again. Reta Baby was due in February with the defensive line.

Nine-pound Charles Aaron Smith sacked Doc Hansen on February 28, 1945. As you know, Nazi Germany and Japan surrendered; Adolph Hitler committed suicide; and the atomic bombs exploded after the news. Sixteen-months-old Willie Ray, Jr., though, could not say the word brother—he kept saying Bubba . . . Bubba.

CHAPTER 3

I Had to Be Twice As Good

THE BIRTH OF BUBBA SMITH had ended World War II, and coach Franklin, who Willie Ray had replaced, was excused from his duties in Europe. Franklin, who had protected his country from the enemy in a segregated army battalion, was now back in Lufkin with his happy family and his old job. There was only one position, so Coach Smith, who owed his career to the war, resigned and was immediately in demand elsewhere.

A truck moved the Smith family out of the town where the Coach had won four district championships. Mama Smith was up front in the cab with a very colorful seventy-year-old youngster named Moses, who had moved "every Negro in East Texas." Moses knew everything and everybody in his Texas and never stopped singing "Let My People Go" during the two-hour trip.

Six-month-old Bubba enjoyed his first on-the-road shower on that day in 1946. He was in the back of the truck under a tarpaulin with the men, squeezed in between the furniture. Moses had called it before they took off from Lufkin, while the sun shone bright and the sky was clear blue. Clear blue except for a tiny patch of dark clouds to the south. Mama Smith corrected his English, but Moses said, "Dat's de only black thang dat's imporper in dis state!" His skin was blacker than the clouds from the Gulf, and the white hair that encircled his strong face gave him a spiritual look as he pointed toward the heavens. He was right, yes he was. Mother Nature performed on that drive along Highway 96, for the newcomers to Orange. The men were soaked through.

Moses hummed and sang right through that storm, and they arrived safely in their new home town. Moses warned them that Orange was unkind to Negroes, but Willie Ray never had any problems with race. It was something about him that almost forced everyone to relax and trust him.

He had full authority with the team and earned a salary of eighteen hundred dollars a year coaching the Wallace High School Dragons of Orange, Texas. It was Coach Smith's introduction into the Golden Triangle, a trio of cities—Orange, Port Arthur, and the bigger city of Beaumont—which formed a football-crazed territory. His objective was sharp, as was his aim toward excellence.

Knowing that they would see him again, the Smith's bade farewell to Moses and remembered his spirit, for they would need it and use it well. Coach Smith was as careful as any intelligent Negro who didn't want to be lynched was in 1946— careful and determined to win in a city which had known anything but winning.

He began with brutal football training, tough discipline, and love. The novices of Wallace High School began to shape up and listen. For example the game against Liberty Negro High was played without a quarterback. They all had been advised, even Tommy Dee, the quarterback, to be at the school at four o'clock sharp to board the bus. Handsome Tommy decided to walk his sexy girlfriend, Grace, home. He arrogantly told the team captain, "Tell Coach Smith to pick me up in front of Salem Church." Coach Smith and his Dragon bus fumed past the embarrassed youngster, not even slowing for him. The team won the game, 12–0. So much for disobedience.

The year 1947 was a winner, and the Coach made changes slowly but knowingly. The youngsters of Orange won the district championship in football and basketball. They celebrated their victory along with the news that Jackie Robinson had been allowed into American professional sports. Mr. Robinson came from a place called Pasadena, California, but to the Negroes of America, he was their own home boy, and a ray of hope.

In 1948 Wallace High was producing for their coach, as was Georgia. Their first hospital-born child was brought into this world without any problem. Given the moniker Harry James, after the then-popular trumpet player, by the radiantly happy mother, it was abruptly changed by Coach Smith on his return from a road game. Lawrence Edward became the official name of the spirited new addition to the Smith dynasty. Perhaps not so coincidentally, color television was introduced to America the same year. The baby boy was brought home three days later. Upon arrival, four-year-old Bubba demanded to know who this small person, creating all of this commotion was. At that, older brother Willie Ray, Jr., an authority on the subject, attempted to explain that this midget was their new brother and that he would be around for a while. With disgust in his voice and tears in his eyes, the betrayed Bubba blurted out, "Yeah, but how long is he going to stay here? When is he leaving?"

It was 1949, the first year Willie Ray, Jr., now known simply as Junior, and Bubba suited up for a game. The six-year-old and four-year-old athletes appeared as uniformed mascots during every home game. Another coincidence cropped up—a new football league was formed, and the Baltimore Colts were born. The two youngsters, Bubba and Baltimore would combine their talents in the not-too-distant future.

The Wallace Dragons, under Coach Smith's training, were becoming a true powerhouse, and Bubba ran into one. It was a Gulf Christmas morning, and Santa Willie Ray and Georgia Claus had presented their brood with as much as they could afford. Times were still struggling tough. Bubba received a bicycle, and he decided to take it for a fast spin in the Gulf fog. The fog was like a pea-soup blanket on that Savior's birthday, but young Bubba had made up his mind to test-drive his new vehicle. Even at the tender age of eight, when Bubba made decisions, that was it. He chose the trail behind the tiny house for his experimental run. The croaking of the frogs welcomed the happy youngster as he guided his first two-wheeler around the snake-curved trail. Bubba so enjoyed his momentary freedom from walking that he forgot to look at anything but his huge feet in size-11 shoes pedaling the brand-new Schwinn.

His fat face decided, without permission from his brain, to grab onto a hanging piece of jagged tin. The neighbors had forgotten to remove a broken outhouse from behind their house. The tin removed a part of his jaw and his roly-poly body off the bike. He kept his cool, though—a Negro must remain cool in the face of calamity—dragged himself up, scraped the meat from the jagged tin, and walked back home.

Mama Smith was alone in the kitchen, cooking her usual unbelievably sumptuous meal for the family. Humming merrily, she hadn't seen her second son's entrance. On first try he simply told her his problem, but Mama kept on singing "Music Maestro, Please." On second try he showed her his problem: a handful of meat in his fat fist and his tongue poking through the gap in his face. She finally looked, then booked, directly to the floor. A yelp left her throat before she collapsed. Bubba had never seen his mother faint before. He began to believe that maybe something was really wrong. Then it began—after his mother had reacted—the pain.

They were tight, Bubba and his mother, despite his dramatic surprises. Junior was his father's shadow at every practice and game. Baby Lawrence, who by now was nicknamed after the cartoon Baby Huey, was wondering what he had gotten into.

The record and play of the Wallace High team was so delightful to the Orange audience that on the night of the semifinals game, a very appreciative, although segregated, audience showed their feelings. During half time in a game against the Lincoln High Bumblebees, Coach and Georgia Smith were called to the center of the football field, between the Negro fans on the east side and the white fans on the west side of the packed stadium.

The stadium was named after Lutcher Stark, an Orange philanthropist, and there he stood to greet the Coach and his wife. He presented the keys to a new station wagon to the Coach as the car glided on the field. Stark stepped up to the microphone and said, "To you, Coach Smith, we are proud of you for the outstanding work you have done." The crowd stood as one and screamed, roared, and applauded their approval. The youngsters looked at each other in amazement. Mama Smith cried tears of gratitude, and in the stands directly behind them sat Moses, shaking his worn head and smiling as he yelled down, "You've unhardened their hearts, Willie Ray!"

Willie Ray winked at Moses, thanked Stark for his gift. Bubba took his first real look at his father; Junior understood because he had worshipped the Coach, his father, for as long as he could remember. Then there was Baby Huey, who wondered what all the fuss was about. "I knew we were rich," he would say later. "We had all those gold trophies at home, with all the food I wanted, and my father's picture always in the newspaper . . . so what's new?"

Year after year—the winning teams, the family love, and the good times. Georgia was feeding "half the high school every day." The Smith sons had to hustle to get their share of the food. One huge student, the Coach's favorite, Ernie Ladd, ate "half the house," complained the Smith boys. Sometimes ten youngsters were fed football food by the sublime and gracious Mrs. Smith.

Junior, twelve years old and getting a little pushy, needed a little shot to keep him in his place and thus had been renamed by Bubba. Beaver was the new moniker, because of his teeth, and soon all of Orange was informed by his younger brother. Nevertheless Beaver remained in charge, and what he said was the law for his middle brother. So when war was declared on Typpy, a sixteen-year-old niggah and his niggah friends, Bubba was ready. (Let us pause for a definition of the word *niggah:* the name Negroes, and only Negroes, could mockingly call themselves, usually in fun and usually to mean *tough*. The other word, the one that white people coined for dark-skinned people, the word *nigger,* means, when used for either white or black people, what it was originally intended to mean: *the worst form of creature.*) Typpy and war—when it rained in Orange, the back yard became gunky mud. Mix the mud with a few rocks, throw them at anyone, and you have the game war.

The boundaries were agreed upon, and the game began. Beaver called the play. "You get up and throw, and when Typpy jumps up to return fire, I'll nail the niggah." Bubba agreed and waited for the signal while a few rocks landed close to his chubby body. "Go!" screamed Beaver, and into action went Bubba. Three rocks flew from his hand toward the enemy. Beaver bolted up and fell back in a instant. A good-sized rock was imbedded in his forehead. "I thought he was dead!" says Bubba now.

"You killed my brother!" screamed the now-serious Bubba. "I went crazy, leaped over a fence, and continued to scream, 'You killed my brother!' When I reached Typpy and his gang, they kicked my ass good!" He left his prone brother in the rain; Bubba's nose, forehead, ribs, and ass had been rearranged without plan. "I told Mother that Typpy had killed Beaver with a rock." A hysterical Mama Smith dashed out into the rain, and Typpy and his friends split. When she saw her first-born son lying in the mud with a rock in his forehead, she fainted again.

The revived Beaver and Bubba carried their mother into the house. Baby Huey enjoyed the excitement as well as the rock still in Beaver's skull. Coach Smith, arriving home from practice, broke both their asses good.

It was the third game of the season for the Coach, and spectators from every city in southwest Texas filled the stadium beyond capacity. It was that way for every Lincoln-Wallace game. The fans screamed themselves hoarse; the bands competed to see who could play louder; and the cheerleaders leaped higher than their opposition. It seemed to get better every time the Wallace High School Dragons played. This was it, the rivalry between Port Arthur and Orange.

The score was 13–13 at half time, and when the teams returned to the playing field, the ovation sounded like a clap of thunder. The third quarter was a defensive battle, and neither team scored. Midway through the fourth quarter the Dragons intercepted a Lincoln pass and drove into the end zone for the winning touchdown.

Orange was in the palm of Coach Smith's hand just when a new principal entered the school, Mr. T. L. Ingram. The former principal's chair was not cold before Ingram began making changes, abrupt changes that frustrated the staff and the students. The one change that he really desired but couldn't achieve was the hero's name: Ingram instead of Smith. A problem was in its embryonic stage, but Coach Smith smiled tantalizingly, and peace prevailed, at least for the moment.

The boys, Beaver, Bubba, and Baby Huey lived, breathed, and slept football. A 5:00 AM wake-up for a quick discussion of the new play created during the Coach's dreams was not unusual, and what was wonderful for the family was that the Coach always asked his wife and the boys for opinions. If their suggestions sounded good, he would use them the very next chance he got. The Coach subtly forced his family to know football and basketball as well as he knew them.

Peer pressure in a Negro neighborhood was, and is, extreme. Toughness was in; vulnerability and sensitivity were out.

Bubba Smith had watched a Negro branded with a burning iron as if he were a steer. He hid behind a bush in North Orange and listened to the screams, smelled the hot flesh, and saw five men burn the letters KKK in a human being's chest. He wanted to remove himself from that pain; he needed to hear other sounds and smell other scents.

He witnessed a demonstration of brass horns in his class

the very next day. He was fascinated. Mama Smith was thrilled when Bubba asked if he could try a saxophone. A balanced education for all of her sons was a never-ending dream of hers. So Roly-poly Bubba used every evening that wasn't football practice to experiment on his new discovery, the sound of music. The melodious squeals of America's next Charlie Parker or Coltrane, in the person of Charles Aaron "Bubba" Smith, oozed out of the school band room.

One evening, when he had just about mastered a scale, a few of his street partners, the niggers of Orange, eased into the room. What did they discover but the football coach's son hunched over his shining ax, wailing away the pain of what he had seen just weeks before. They jealously busted up, broke down, howled sideways, and called Master Smith every name they could invent, mostly ending or beginning with the magic negative of all ghettoes, *faggot*.

He has never been called that again—nor has he ever tried to play the sax again.

Willie Ray, Jr., was not experimenting with sounds; he was testing his body, alone, on a football field. He did not want any one to see him, as clumsy as he was, until he was ready.

Baby Huey was growing up. He was brought to the rice canal, as his brothers had been, for swimming lessons. Coach had a rare Sunday off, and Mama had taken time from her studies for her master's degree. It was a muggy, tranquil Texas day, normal for a seacoast town. Mama Smith sat on the bridge with her shoes off, watching her two oldest sons diving and swimming beneath her. Coach Smith began his lessons, and Baby Huey smiled, content to be in the spotlight for a change.

The competition between Beaver and Bubba increased for the rice canal championship, and Baby Huey's lessons improved. Suddenly Mama let out a wail that might have awakened President Eisenhower from a golf lesson. She had seen a snake in the canal. A big, oily, nasty reptile in the same water where her sons were playing. Georgia's alarm threw her off balance, and she fell from the bridge. She grabbed a huge nail on the side of the wooden span and held on for dear life. At the very moment of her fall Bubba was emerging from an underwater spin directly beneath his mother. They connected, and her falling weight drove him down into the mud below the canal.

They all reacted to her alarm. Beaver and Willie Ray to the

rescue! Baby Huey forgot for the moment that he was a novice and splashed his way toward his mother. They were all there now, next to her, holding her. All there except Bubba, who had remained beneath the water as a footstool. Now safe, she screamed again, "My God, my dress is up." Everyone laughed except the nearly drowned Bubba.

There was more than one lady on Bubba's brain. The sex drive had stampeded into the long, uneventful life of nine-year-old Charles Aaron Smith. It had rolled over his mind, squashed his nerves, and left him helpless.

He was helpless, and she was Georgia Mae Finney. Fine Georgia Mae Finney, s-o-o-o fine! A hope-to-die love had sacked his heart. "She had that long, silky black hair, down to here; those high cheek bones; honey-toned butter-velvet skin; hazel eyes; and a mouth that made you swallow hard. Just thinking about her made my mind stammer!" Smith says he had it bad.

There was only one problem—there always is. Georgia Mae Finney, age 8½, gave up nothing but the ol' ig, *ig* for *ignore,* and Georgia Mae was late even with an acknowledgment of Bubba's existence.

"I had to have a plan," says Bubba. "It was like a football play, maybe the flea flicker, or the end around—well, I knew it was a game on her part. It had to be, and she played it well. Most of the other girls couldn't stay away from me," he says proudly.

"Now, I had the best partner, his given name was Earl Zetar, and I called him Time. Time was so cool. I was the class clown. Time laughed at all my jokes, all the time, on time. Time was cool. We both were on the chubby side. His mother cooked her ass off. Time was cool."

It happened one day in the school cafeteria, that magic moment when you hear the violins and feel the fireworks exploding in your knees. They met, these two healthy Afro-Americans came together in one spot in this huge world, next to the pea-soup bowls. "Cool Time was with me. I stared at Georgia for a long minute and then began talking my talk. She made believe she wasn't listening, but I knew better. All I could see in my mind's eye was me holding Georgia Mae Finney and kissing her. Man, she was fine!"

Most elegant eight-year-old females who understand what Mother Nature has done for them negotiate. They will not fall for the first move. Georgia was elegant, so she passed on Bubba's B material. He offered to give her the pleasure of his kiss. "I'll only kiss you if your friend kisses Ingrid," she shot back, smiling at her blushing friend. "I hadn't noticed Ingrid, but there she was, and there she was, and there she was, all of her standing to the right of Georgia." Bubba was thinking Alpo when he looked toward Ingrid. "But my partner," he goes on, "was Time, and Time was cool. I turned to him and repeated her offer. Time looked at me, then at Ingrid. I grinned at fine Georgia, then back at Time. My ace boon was shaking his head no. I couldn't believe it; he must have misunderstood. This was life or death, I reminded him." Time thought, Bubba's life and my death, so he bowed his head and booked. "My man had refused, turned me down, played me off, and kicked my behind in one moment. Time was uncool." Georgia Mae Finney remained fine as she turned on her heel and walked away. Damn! Bubba froze in heart-broken agony, humiliated.

It was 1955, and in another part of America, Rosa Parks, a mild-mannered Montgomery, Alabama, seamstress had refused to give up her seat on a bus to a white man. The black revolution had begun.

The only thing that had begun in Orange was another day. The annual summer vacation for Beaver, Bubba, and Baby Huey in beautiful, boring Nacogdoches was enforced. Georgia's loving but stern mother was their foreman for four long weeks. Nannie Lonie they called her, and she was ruthlessly in charge of their actions. Every night was church, and when they weren't at church, the church was at the house—and they all adored Baby Huey's cute cheeks. When the perfumed, powdered, and paunchy ladies pinched the youngster's face, he had to maintain his patience or Nanny would go to work on his other cheeks. These were the choice's he had—none and none.

One bright morning Uncle George offered the boys a job shucking corn. The same morning had brought news that a circuit preacher, the good Reverend Amos, had stopped next door, and in three days was on his way in his '47 Oldsmobile to Louisiana. "The way to Louisiana from Nacogdoches was through Orange," thought a very clever and inventive Beaver. "We could take the jobs, get the cash, pay Rev's gas bill, and be home in three days." Bubba agreed instantly. He always saw eye to eye with his oldest brother. There was something about Beaver that made most people go along with his ideas.

The job was a grueling twelve hours a day for three steaming days, plagued by Texas mosquitoes that must have trained under Coach Smith. They were truly dragons and proved it every chance they got. It was worth it, however, so Beav and Bub thought—anything to get out of Nacogdoches.

Lawrence Edward, better known as Baby Huey, wondered what had happened to his brothers' brains for taking those jobs. He knew them and wondered hard.

They worked with a passion, without complaint. Two brothers shucking corn like veterans. Sometimes a smile would pass between them as the hours passed. It was finally over: their hands were blistered and their backs ached; but they had worked together for freedom. Uncle George praised their efforts as he paid them—fifty cents for each and three giant watermelons. The boys could only wonder about their uncle's sanity. Seventy-two hours of kiss-my-ass hard work for one dollar and some melons, they thought, stunned by the reality of their wages. "I hope you have severe chest pains!" said Bubba. "And unending diarrhea," added Beaver, and they stalked away from their open-mouthed uncle.

Home now, they discussed the agony of their defeat. Baby Huey was in the bathroom, a wall away from their words, and all he heard was the sentence "We gotta split," and all he knew was that no one had invited him. He immediately ran to his Nanny and told her what he had overheard. For his information he received ten of Nanny Lonie's severest blows with a peach limb, and Lawrence Edward Smith learned a lesson and never squealed on his brothers again.

Bubba's hero-worshipping of Beaver began that summer—while eating six giant watermelons.

Back home, watching brother Beaver prepare himself for his football career, Bubba saw the improvement and wondered about his own future. He wasn't sure what he wanted to do with his life. His father had not demanded a football career, not really, but there was an underlying notion that there might be a whole lot less food if he didn't.

The Coach had attained more than he had hoped for in Orange, but he wasn't being helped by the new principal, Ingram, and his nerves were strained by what he considered to be childish jealousy.

Meanwhile Bubba's confusion became focused in mischief in junior high school. He decided to try his hand at business. Why not the treasurer? Not much labor in being a treasurer, and the pay was up to him. He formed a social club with seven youngsters. He graciously allowed them entrance into his club after they had payed him dues. He would give each enough cash so that they wouldn't starve, and he would keep the rest. Twenty-five dollars and two weeks later the only problem was the nosy parents of his club members. They had discovered the brilliant plan when their children began to faint from starvation.

The phone rang at the Smith's home, and the Coach heard of his son's industry. When Bubba returned from school that afternoon, his father was waiting. Bubba didn't have to wait long before an explanation was requested. He immediately went on the defensive and began with a flurry of man-this and man-that. "Where did you learn that kind of talk?" demanded the Coach, reaching for his board of education. Willie Ray had a small two-by-four in his back pocket. Though it was usually reserved for his football players, it seemed to be needed to teach his son a lesson or two. His board was personalized: COACH SMITH was engraved upon it. "Bubba's speed was improving," Willie Ray laughs. "He scooted under the daybed and caught hold to the springs. I was about to beat the black off him, but he wouldn't move. I had to kneel down and swing. Bubba just held on to the springs as we slid across the room and back again. I almost had a heart attack."

Coach Smith survived, and Bubba's first venture into the business world was at an end.

Lawrence Edward was growing up, and he joined his brothers in driving their parents crazy. He lived in the movie house, down on John and Second Street. Having witnessed his brothers' moves, he acknowledged that they were inventive but insisted they lacked style. He, on the other hand, had a movie idol who exuded style from each and every pore. Fred Astaire was his name, and Baby Huey copied his game. The way Astaire moved, even the way he put out his cigarettes, impressed the young Smith.

He was attempting to teach his brothers style at home on one of those east Texas rainy days. When it rained in those Gulf cities, it looked as if the entire Gulf was being poured slowly over the houses. The boys were stuck indoors and were steadily pushing their nearly berserk mother over the edge. So much so that Georgia informed Coach Smith, upon his soaked arrival from practice, of their behavior. The Coach was tired and wet, but he knew that when his wife called for help, it was an emergency. He ordered all three of his growing boys into the bathroom—"where there was nothing to hide under."

As he removed the board from his back pocket, he looked directly into the eyes of his elder boys, Beaver and Bubba. He recognized for the first time that both boys had a familiar look behind their eyes. It was the same look that he had had when he was their age. It was hopeless, he knew. So he excused his two young men, now thirteen and eleven, and motioned his eight-year-old to stay. "You two are completely crazy; but I can save you, Lawrence!"

Lawrence could not believe his eyes as Beaver and Bubba, without a word of defense or compassion for their little brother, strolled quietly out of the bathroom. He seized his time, stood abruptly from his crouched position next to the tiled wall, and announced, "I'm crazier than they ever will be, Coach!"

Coach couldn't hold it in. He dropped to his knees, bellowing with laughter of such intensity that he could not speak. Beaver and Bubba were rolling around on the floor outside, laughing their asses off. Mama Smith could only put her hands to her hips, sigh, and shake her head. Her husband and three sons were hopeless, pitiful, and wonderful.

That is how it was on a daily basis with the Smiths. Laughter was necessary, constant, even mandatory. Anyone remaining depressed more than one hour had to be sick enough for immediate hospitalization. Friendship and food were the only indulgences allowed; any other and the family would be on your case until you relented. They all spoiled each other rotten.

Besides his eight district and two state football championships, one basketball championship and his seventy-seven football victories, a crippled Negro high school coach named Smith was glowingly praised by the Houston *Post Parade* in their Sunday edition. It was an in-depth story of "how he had worked with his athletes, teachers, parents, and law enforcement people in lessening crime and juvenile delinquency in Orange." The article went on to say, "While there was hatred occurring throughout the world, blacks and whites were paying homage to a Negro coach for outstanding work in the community."

The publicity was sensational for Willie Ray, but Principal Ingram was annoyed. The mood became even worse when Charlton Pollard High in Beaumont inquired regarding the Coach's future. Coach Smith, before accepting or rejecting the offer, tried again to get the full support of his principal. He advised Ingram that he was injuring the students by not backing proposals for equipment and other necessities. An irate Ingram called Willie Ray Smith a damn liar to his face, and the shit hit the fan. Minutes before, Willie Ray had taken a knife away from a student, one of the hundred picketing the school chanting, "Fire Ingram; hire Smith." An excited Coach Smith didn' draw the knife, yet he did chase the screaming principal out of his office, down the hall, and into a bathroom. Sitting on a stool in the very same bathroom was Ernie Ladd— six-foot eight-inch Ernie Ladd, the Coach's favorite and the star of the Wallace High School Dragons. Ernie leaped to his huge feet, his pants still down around his size-18 shoes, and lifted Willie Ray over his head, suggesting that the Coach change his plans. Ernie Ladd, who eventually became one of the giants of the National Football League, had accomplished an amazing feat by this act. He had singlehandedly saved Principal Ingram a life; Coach Smith a career; Georgia Smith a husband; and their children a father.

Bubba, unaware, was in class while all of this activity was going on, but he had heard the shouting pickets rooting for his father. He was, coincidently, in Principal Ingram's wife's class. As he stood to gain a better vantage point, Mrs. Ingram slapped him back into his chair. Bubba pushed her across the room with one motion and left the classroom, joining the pickets and his exhausted father. Coach Smith was busy telling the pickets, "Stop, turn around, and go back to your education. I'm leaving Orange." They cried unashamedly for their friend and teacher. "The ballplayers dug him, the students admired him, and I loved him like I had never loved him before, that last day at Wallace," recalls Bubba.

Ol' Moses and the Smith men loaded up his wooden truck for what was to be the Smith's final move as a family. Each of them sensed the importance of the moment. Everyone, although working together, was into themselves, thinking only of their own future. Georgia, of course, directed the loading of the truck. She had grown into a brilliant, subtle general over these Orange years. Coach Willie Ray hoorahed—Black Texan for roasted—their sons, who were learning the hoorah craft from the master. "Don't be afraid to lift anything heavy, Beaver!" he would say whenever his oldest son took a break. Beaver remained intense and beyond everyone. Bubba was a blotter—he considered everything his mother, father, or brother said or did, and used what worked. Baby Huey, now eight, was working on his style.

The citizens of Orange, all except Principal Ingram, his wife, and the Ku Klux Klan, had turned out to wish them well. The ladies, dressed in their Sunday-go-to-meetin' clothes, brought Georgia their best dishes. The men traded their funniest, proudest stories with the Coach; and the Wallace boys, without a coach, shuffled from foot to foot, jealous of the Smith boys. The girls, except Georgia Mae Finney, were thoroughly pissed.

The green, spanking-clean Buick carried the family, except Bubba, in comfort. James Brown weeped on the radio. Bubba rode in the truck with Moses, listening to stories about slaves running away, rebelling—"And we didn't have no place to run to. My pappy ran away, 1848."

Bubba listened carefully to Moses. "Can you imagine what this ol' Negro had to go through?" he asked. Bubba shook his head no. "Can you imagine," he continued, "the day a Negro woman went to her man and said, 'Honey, I'm pregnant,' and both of 'em fell on der knees and prayed dat de child be born deformed. Can you imagine what dis Negro went through, hoping his own baby is crippled? You see, Bubba, if he was born cripple, he would have less chance of being a slave and more chance of havin' freedom. Think about dat, boy, think about how lucky you are to be healthy. Times is bad, but it ain't like it was, nah, sir. Bubba, be proud you's healthy and never, ever forget dat you free!" He mixed these stories with his favorite hymn, "Let My People Go!"

Beaumont is the largest city the Smiths had lived in, its population 113,000 in 1957. A port on the Neches River, it was now home.

President Eisenhower had had to send the 101st Airborne Division to escort nine black children into Little Rock's Central High School, but no one had to escort Willie Ray Smith into Beaumont's Charlton Pollard High School. The school was wall-to-wall Negroes, and the Coach was the HNIC, the Head-Negro-in-Charge. With his assistant, Arthur Randall, who sounded like a foghorn, the Coach laid down the rules.

1. NO FOOTBALL PLAYERS ARE TO BE ON THE STREET AFTER 9:00 PM.

2. SMOKING WILL NOT BE TOLERATED.
3. DRINKING OF ALCOHOLIC BEVERAGES OF ANY KIND WILL NOT BE TOLERATED.
4. THE USE OF PROFANITY ON AND OFF THE FIELD WILL NOT BE TOLERATED.
5. DAILY ATTENDANCE AT ALL PRACTICE SESSIONS AND CLASSES IS MANDATORY.
6. THEFT WILL NOT BE TOLERATED.
7. PLAYERS WILL BE GIVEN A SET OF OFFENSIVE PLAYS. EACH PLAYER IS REQUIRED TO KNOW HIS ROLE IN EACH PLAY. THIS IS VERY IMPORTANT.
8. HORSEPLAY IN THE LOCKER ROOM WILL NOT BE TOLERATED.
9. THE COACHING STAFF HOPES THAT THIS SEASON WILL BE A SUCCESSFUL ONE. THE ONLY WAY IT CAN BE IS TO WORK TOGETHER. SPEED, BLOCKING, AND TACKLING ARE IMPORTANT ASPECTS OF FOOTBALL, BUT TO BECOME A GREAT FOOTBALL PLAYER, ONE MUST MAKE A *SACRIFICE*.

MOTTO: ONE FOR ALL, ALL FOR ONE—A TEAM THAT WON'T BE BEAT CANNOT BE BEAT.

That ancient sin, envy, began to raise its ugly head when a slow but learning Willie Ray Smith, Jr., was chosen by his father to play wide receiver on offense and linebacker on defense. Nepotism was the cry from students uncertain of the invaders from Orange.

In another world, at the same time, a motion picture was filming in Hollywood, starring Sidney Poitier. *The Defiant Ones* was about men who, although prisoners, fought back; but in some cities in 1957 Negroes had accepted their prison, and in some cities it was a no-changes-please attitude. Beaumont was one of those cities, and some at Charlton Pollard High School, chronic losers, resisted change of any sort. Some people worship slavery and use it as an excuse for mediocrity. Coach Smith never understood or accepted slavery, mediocrity or losing.

Coach Smith didn't demand radical change. The football team lacked the spirit of winning, and his initial goal was to instill it in them. When his team of novices lost, 100–0, in an early game, the Coach was confused and bitter even after discovering that the other coach had stacked his team with ringers from a nearby army base.

He took a long walk that autumn Monday along the tranquil

Neches waterfront. He limped along, his disability constantly reminding him of his own courage, and he grew angry at himself. His objective, now gnawing at him, was to find a way to motivate these truly crippled young men who accepted defeat, but he had tried, he thought, every imaginable way. Nothing seemed to work. He had never experienced this problem in smaller towns. Could it be that large cities mauled the spirit? Was it that he could not teach sophisticated youngsters? What was the answer?

The glittering water reflected the new sun, and it seemed to beckon him. He moved toward its edge, kneeled down, and saw his own image in the river. He stared at the fleeting mirror and suddenly saw another reflection standing squarely beside him. It was his namesake, his son, Willie Ray, Jr., and he felt an arm around his shoulder. "You were the one who told us never to quit, to see it through!" Beaver said. They looked at each other and cried together, these two bronze Americans, in a city in East Texas, seventeen hundred miles from fantasy, each a hero. All they seemed to need was their friendship.

The very next year it began—talent burst forth. Beaver had honed his physical machine to a fine edge that spring. Basketball, track, and hours of football homework had consumed him. He was arrogantly bright.

The Coach sat his three sons down one practice day and advised them, "If you're going to play for me, you must be twice as good as the kids competing against you!" They looked at each other; only Beaver was mature enough to understand.

Unlike Beaver, Bubba wasn't the least sure of himself in either his studies or his sports. He also discovered that he was nearsighted, a problem in basketball, though not in football, where everything was close-up. And so he dreamed of blocking for his talented brother when he reached high school. Beyond that, no plans were made; most of his time was spent around the house, watching his mother and adoring the quickness of her mind. He became Beaver's private shoeshine boy and chief shoelace washer. He knew his older brother was ready: he watched him practice daily.

"Chubby little Lawrence Edward was in elementary school, but his mind was anything but, as he began designing plays for his delighted father. His L Formation was accepted one dawn family meeting, and the next week the play was used with startling success, startling even to Baby Huey.

The 1959 season opened with a burst of lightning. Willie Ray, Jr., fielded the opening kickoff and weaved his way seventy-two yards through eleven shocked young men for a touchdown. On the first play from the line of scrimmage, he streaked sixty-two yards for another six points. Charlton Pollard won their first game, 52–12, with Master Smith scoring five touchdowns.

He was now irrevocably in charge of his talent. When they played Booker T. Washington High of Houston, Beaver asked his coach and father for a twenty-second rest. It was the fourth quarter, and the teams were deadlocked, 0–0. He also said, "When I return, I'll win this game for you, Coach!" On the very first play after his blow, he intercepted a Washington pass and glided seventy yards to the opponents' twenty-yard line. Georgia, his mother, seated behind the team bench, screamed in happiness. The next play saw him scoot the remaining yards for a touchdown. Georgia wailed in joy. His run was called back on an offside penalty. Georgia booed the referee and loudly questioned his heritage. Baby Huey's L Formation play was called, and Beaver carried the ball into the end zone with unbelievable ease. Georgia let loose a howl of pleasure and fainted, of course.

Bubba had a new hero, Lawrence began working on some new plays, and Coach Smith was the proudest man in the Lone Star State.

Charlton Pollard beat Yates, Wheatley, Kashmere, Oldine, and Worthy high schools that season, and Beaver ran winning touchdowns in every game. Beaver, now called Willie Ray "Doll," Jr., was also scoring with the ladies, and his popularity was playing tricks with his memory. It must have been—he knew that 11:00 PM was in-the-house time. It was after a big football victory, so the Coach relaxed a little and waited patiently.

"Sweetheart, do you think he might have been injured?" Georgia began to bug her husband about Beaver's whereabouts around 1:00 AM, and he was out of bed, down the stairs, and behind the door in ten seconds, despite his limp.

The entire family was awake when the young lady's voice sounded, "Goodnight, Beaver, and thanks!" Beaver replied, "Goodnight, Zenobia." Georgia grew more nervous, Bubba worried, and Lawrence was exploding with the excitement of the moment. They heard Beaver's footsteps resound on the pavement as the car pulled away. Beaver's memory returned about this time, and he belatedly recalled his curfew. His secure footfalls ceased, and he tiptoed to the door. The key was in, and his hand was poised on the doorknob. The sensitive son sensed danger but he did not know how or whence it would come. The door eased open. Bubba by this time was desperately trying to warn his brother of their father's presence directly behind the opening door.

Beaver didn't have time to see the signal; a naked fist moved quickly toward his jaw. The impact sent him sprawling against the wall. The lights were on now, and so was Georgia. She floated grandly down the stairs toward her husband and fallen son. The Coach was in the middle of a lecturing ass-kicking. Each blow was followed by "I told you never . . . ." Bubba was transfixed, and Baby Huey was taking bets on how long Beaver would remain conscious.

It was Mama who ended the slaughter. She had remembered her Nacogdoches singing voice and began an improvised opera, lyrics of which began "That's enough, Sweetheart, that's enough." Like most of these spankings, it ended with laughter. Willie Ray was exhausted anyway, but his wife's aria sent him into a rolling hysteria. Beaver, brought back to reality, became a fancier of his mother's singing talent.

The final game of the season was a family affair. Charlton Pollard was losing. It was half time, and Bubba heard the whistle—a familiar sound—not the referee's, but Mama's. All of the Smith's knew the tune. The five-foot eight-inch Bubba raced as fast as his size-fourteen shoes would carry him from the players bench to her seat in the stands. She kissed her son and gave him a folded note for the Coach. "Take this to your father, sweetheart." Down the steps waddled Bubba to the locker room and his father. He was in the middle of a pep-up lecture when Bubba handed him the paper. He read it and hit Bubba on top of his head. "Never bring a note from your mother, again!" he shouted at the innocent young man. Bubba walked away muttering to himself.

The first play the Coach used in the second half was the play that Georgia had suggested in her informal letter. It of course featured Beaver, and he ran for a thirty-eight yard touchdown. Everyone on the team knew where the play had come from, but no one seemed to have the courage to say so out loud. It was all the points Charlton Pollard needed to win. The Smiths were working as a team.

It was 1959—a massive, well-structured revolution for American Negroes was growing stronger. While this electric activity raced through our country, Bubba Smith slept. When he awoke, he stuffed himself with any and all food in the household. When this stage of his life began, he was five feet eight inches tall and weighed nearly one hundred ninety pounds. He was fourteen and was entering Charlton Pollard High School. Four months after it began, he was six feet eight and two hundred seventy pounds. "I couldn't stay awake," he says. "My clothes were getting small, but I didn't realize what exactly was happening to me."

The Coach's family, as well as Georgia's, was large, but their son's flash growth was unexpected. Big Bubba began to coordinate his new self the spring of 1960. He was preparing to join his brother and father at Charlton Pollard High School. The stretching and spreading of his body had leveled off, and his speed began to improve. They ran every night, working for both quickness and sweetness. "Think sweet," Coach Smith instructed, and the clumsy fat kid began to transform himself into the beginnings of a fluid junior giant with style.

CHAPTER 4

Grab Everybody, Sort, Toss, 'Til I Find the One with the Ball—Keep Him!

A MAN CAN BE ENERGIZED by hunger, and any pain in his heart or disorder in his brain will vanish if he believes his hunger is about to be relieved—especially if the object of his craving is not lemon pie or lobster but gold. What would happen, do you think, if a teenager were offered gold over love? A Negro youngster whose grandparents were bought and sold with gold and lived on little else but love should know better than others; or he might be more accessible to the gold givers, since he needs it, he thinks, more than others.

Some of the very same young men who had accepted food, understanding, teaching, friendship, and love from the Smiths of Beaumont accepted cash money not only to throw a high school football game but to allow a near-fatal injury to their star teammate, Willie Ray Smith, Jr.

The star part was most of the problem. Beaver, as well as his father, was solidly in the spotlight of Beaumont. The star spot is a place that most people only dare to dream about. Most refuse to work to get there, and others bitterly realize it is not their destiny.

An adult in the city of Beaumont, who may have had a son playing on the team, burned with the pitiful sin of envy. He had to be in the chips—a professional man, with cash to burn and trinkets to give away. Like a powerful crab in a barrel of crabs, he dragged down those who would dare to escape from the barrel—he dragged them down with him, where everyone belonged.

It happened one tepid Texas day in Marshall, with eighteen thousand citizens watching a crippled football coach discipline thirty-three young men in a team sport. Willie Ray "Beaver" Smith, Jr., was ready for posterity that day, and he knew it. Some athletes rise to occasions; some stretch their talent; but few are the possessors of a natural brilliance, like this man-boy. Everyone could feel it—from the bouncy driver who drove the team bus to the teen-age girls who pined for his look, they felt it. Even nature knew it—have you ever seen a rainbow without the rain? The rainbow pointed to a hanging cloud that drifted above Dillon Stadium that Saturday in 1960.

"I want to fly, not run," Beaver said, his tawny eyes staring beyond the crowded, noisy grandstands. His biggest fan, brother Blubber Bubba, had joined the Smith–Charlton Pollard dynasty that semester and was learning how to use his new body to open holes in other teams. The fallen bodies were used as mats for his so-sweet flying running brother, number 44.

The game began, and a fan who had driven his truck up from Beaumont leaned over to one of his drinking buddies and said, "The police had to escort the niggah to and from the stadium in Boomahnt. He would score a touchdown, and the bitches went berserk. He score another, and sheeet, they would rush on to the field after his black ass! The boy is as lucky as I am bald." They all laughed and passed the Thunderbird. The scouts, sitting in the white section, could hear him fifty yards away, and they licked their lips.

It was high school fun, and a day-off-from-the-man kind of day.

Number 44 went beyond the dreams of men six minutes after the game started. He moved through Bubba's block, broke two tackles on his own, and flew.

Three touchdowns were flown that game, all of them called because of inexcusable infractions committed by his angelic-looking teammates. Simplistic errors by the trained athletes that surrounded his unbelieving, tearful brother Bubba—errors never committed before this game. They had this here way of standing, all the brothers did, a Boomahnt Smith Stance, with hands on their hips, one foot a few inches in front of the other, and a cool calm on their faces. Beaver stood that way after each of his scores, as if waiting for the penalty. He sensed the ugly, smelled the nigger in the fresh woodpile, and sauntered back, looking at his teammates, wondering who it was. He looked at his brother, who could only pat his own leg, nervously wondering along with his brother.

During the third quarter—Charlton Pollard behind by six—Satan struck with a fury. Beaver was hit from behind, ten seconds after the whistle signaling the end of the play blew. His million-dollar knee was torn, and his scream ran right up that rainbow.

"They couldn't deal," says Bubba. "Beaver was making everyone else look so bad that they went crazy."

What they did deal was pain for gold. A yellow metal for an athlete's career. "What they couldn't erase, no matter who it was or what they did, was the unbelievable talent of my brother!" Bubba says.

The players could not look the Coach, Beaver, or Bubba directly in the eye that day. It did not help the crippled Coach's anguish; he already knew what friends can do to each other. The scouts, however, still panted for Beaver's services, despite the injury. "That damn thing'll heal. Willie Ray is a strong boy!" one said as he scrambled for an interview that next week. One hundred one scholarships were offered him at season's end. Bubba was impressed by the few dollars he made lining up interviews for the scouts with Beaver.

Baby Huey's unending showmanship made them all howl. He played football, with a passion, and had happily gained a new nickname. Baby Huey no longer seemed to suit the roughhousing, crowd-pleasing lover boy, now age 14. The female members of his Spanish class at Dunbar Junior High, after seeing him play football, swooned and dubbed him El Toro, soon changed to Tody. What he gave each of the females is another story.

It was the basketball game of the semester, and every Negro, niggah, and nigger, and every other colored folk, was in the Dunbar gymnasium that evening. The Smith clan sat near the center line. The teams warmed up, and Tody showed off a few of his moves to Carol, who sat above the home team bench, to Gina, who sat above the visiting team bench, to Patricia, who sat near one basket, and to Claudine, who sat near the other. One of his more dramatic, Academy Award–winning moves brought the entire audience to their feet screaming with laughter.

When Tody jogged stylishly back to the center line, his partner Sparky tapped him on the shoulder and called him over with a beckoning finger. "Not now," shouted Tody, who was fired up. The fans, including his father and brothers, were crying now, some next to stomach-aching hysteria. Tody could not for the life of him understand the reaction, but he never could understand his audience—he just owned it. Finally Spanky whispered in his ear, a whisper Bubba could hear where he sat, and it caused him to fall off his bench seat. "Your balls are hanging out," Spanky said. "Wot you say?" Tody was unable to hear Spanky above all this silly laughter. Sparky, sensing his moment, screamed the words, and the gymnasium roared. Tody looked down. His last Earl the Pearl move had ripped his shorts and his jockstrap both, with the obvious result.

Georgia was walking toward him now, her hand over her mouth, her body gyrating like a jackhammer. "Come, son," she said, a needle and thread already in hand. "Come, son, let Mama fix that." Georgia Smith is five feet four inches tall, and Tody, at 14, was nearing six and weighed close to two hundred. Georgia took his hand and walked him back to her classroom, where she taught economics at Dunbar, and sewed up his jockstrap and his shorts in time for the game.

When they returned to the gymnasium, a standing ovation ensued. Tody scored twenty-four points that night—he had something going for him that game: when he drove to the basket, the defending players, remembering his pregame exhibition laughed hard enough to allow Mr. Smith to get a step on them. Dunbar won by fourteen points.

One of Beaver's scholarship offers came from Michigan State University. The offer was easily engineered by Sweetheart Smith when he attended a Texas high school coaching clinic in Dallas. When Beaver's exploits were described at lunch one day, Duffy Daugherty, coach at Michigan State, became intrigued and made an offer. Beaver turned it down in favor of another, from Iowa. He had visited Iowa and loved the feel of the school; the possibilities opened up by the prospect of his playing there; and the Negro students at Iowa, who seemed refreshingly intelligent and sophisticated. Burned in Beaumont by lower form, he decided on Iowa. And it was at Iowa he first heard John Coltrane. A student from Philadelphia named Wesley hipped him to the sound, the sound of Coltrane.

The New Frontier, Freedom Rides, and change in America 1961. Texas's own Lyndon Johnson became the Vice President of the United States of America. Ol' Lyndon, like most good Texans, lived down the road a piece. Mr. Vice President was from, of all places, Johnson City. Some New Englander, an Irish Catholic, a first, became President.

John F. Kennedy's inaugural speech includes the sentence "Ask not what your country can do for you; ask what you can do for your country." Bubba Smith said almost the same thing to the Charlton Pollard team, but used the word *coach* instead of *country*.

He had become the leader of the team. The players, now jealous of him, the Coach's son, the captain, made him pay for the honor by egging him into becoming the team chauffeur. Bubba hated driving but consented. Every chance he got, he forced himself to be one of the boys; of course it never worked. He hung with his new running buddy, George Egland, and taught himself even to smoke cigarettes—just to belong. He refused, though, to drink or to take drugs: "It didn't make any sense."

The Coach remained a strict disciplinarian and went on prowls after curfew. One minute after the time he had set, 9:00 PM, he was out "lookin' to see if the rules were being respected," his fingers wrapped around his board of education. Once he drove through black Boomahnt, taking the grain truck route behind the pool halls and the Dew Drop Inn. Seeing his cornerback, Harvey Brown, on the street, checking things out with the get-down cats, he stopped his car and eased up to the group. He was highly respected—everyone knew the Coach. They spotted him, and they walked away, leaving behind trembling Harvey.

The cigarette, sucked on moments before, had disappeared instantly. Coach knew all the tricks—he'd seen the same in Lufkin, Orange, and now Boomahnt, the cittay. The lit Pall Mall was in his pants pocket, in the middle of his fist. The Coach had his sadistic moments, and this was certainly one. He folded his arms, rocked back on his good leg, and decided to have a long chat with the sweating player. The chat lasted long enough, and Harvey was scared enough, to have his pants catch fire. Harvey suffered second-degree burns and later a paddling in front of the team.

That next day, it was a hard practice, for Bubba as well as for a teammate who was by then in the hospital having an operation. Bubba was the captain and had to be twice as good, but John Slaughter had injured him. Bubba had used a four-letter word, a few in fact. As they rolled off of his tongue, he knew what would happen; he didn't know how. Then it hit like a clap of thunder. Coach walked on the field and punched him with both fists on both ears. A heavyweight boxing. He turned, walked back to the huddle, heard the players ask for a play. He called one, the team slapped their hands together, and moved into position. Bubba looked at Slaughter; actually he looked through him. He heard the hut-hut and the ball snapped, and Bubba threw a forearm that ripped John's lower jaw embedding his teeth beneath his tongue. Practice was ended then, and George Egland, his partner, joined Bubba. Yes, it had been a hard practice.

They were double-dating, George and Bub, whenever Bubba could talk his father out of the family automobile. "We were having a real nice time, ol' George and I." Bubba enjoyed having a friend besides his brothers, a refreshing experience. They were running tight, hanging tough, until the Coach's transmission went bad. As soon as that happened, good ol' George Egland, Bubba's good buddy, went south—he left.

Sensing Bubba's frustration with people and disapproving of his son showing anger toward his teammates, Coach Smith cautioned him. He sat Bubba down one early morning when only the pigeons were moving and lectured his maturing son. "Put your faith in your talent," he said. "Repress your reaction to fools. Save your energy for football, and you'll get a return." Those one hundred painted yards, the goal posts, and the stadium seats would become his only friends until he harnessed his talent.

Another problem was school. It bored him. Once in biology class, he couldn't stop dreaming about football. John Nathan, a smart youngster, the trainer on the football team, kept poking him awake. Today's lesson was frogs and the dissection of those ugly critters. Bubba thought to himself that the frogs looked amazingly like the biology teacher—that analogy and Nathan's nudges kept him from deep sleep. The teacher, sensing Bubba's lack of interest, called on him, and Mr. Smith panicked. He was asked to stand and describe the muscle structure of the leg of the frog. The teacher directed a mute Bubba to the front of the room. As he left his seat, Nathan whispered some words of wisdom his way. He reached the front, behind the table on which a frog laid stretched out as a model, and began repeating the words of his ally, Nathan.

Little Lonnie Bass, the female four-eyed wonder of the eleventh grade, squealed. She openly questioned the source of Bubba's knowledge. Bubba, recalling his father's voice said nothing to Miss Bass but took the blunt knife that was on the table and stuck it into the frog's stomach. The slimmey guts of the reptile accidentally squirted onto Little Lonnie's humongous eyeglasses. The forty-five class members erupted into unrelenting laughter. The teacher froze, but Miss Bass would have none of this treatment. She removed her stained glasses and leaped at the huge young man. She slapped him, as hard as her minature muscles allowed her to.

Blame it on athletic reflexes, if you wish, but the tree trunk referred to as Mr. Smith's arm flew into action. His arm took wing, and Little Lonnie took flight. She moved through the air with the greatest of ease and, plop, Miss Bass was on her ass, and the teacher had lost his class. He went into a rage, as only he could. He commanded the six-foot eight-inch, two-hundrd-seventy-pound hulk out of the room, down the hall, and into the custodial closet. He, like all the teachers at Charlton Pollard, had a board in his back pocket, modeled after Coach Smith's, though without an engraving. He demanded Bubba drop his pants. Now Bubba would have, under normal conditions; this time, though, he refused and accepted the lesser of two evils. A resounding blow hit Bubba in the thigh. He turned and advised his teacher, respectfully, that the blow had accomplished its objective. The teacher did not agree, in the slightest. He raised his fragile arm to strike again; Bubba snatched his arm, lifted his startled teacher into the air, walked out of the closet, his teacher still in hand, to a wastebasket, and dropped him in, headfirst.

No disrespect meant, but the punishment did not fit the crime, Bubba thought. He was taken down to the physical education department, where his father was conversing with his four assistant coaches. When Coach Smith heard the story, he asked his son to comment. Bubba stared off into space. He was ordered to drop his pants and spread-eagle himself against the equipment cage. Coach Smith and his assistants took five licks a piece. "My father seemed to hit the hardest," Bubba recalls. "I remembered his lecture, about whose son I was and what it meant. I had to be twice as good."

His first year as a leader was a learning experience. He centered the ball and opened gaps in the opposing team big enough for a motor home to drive through. Ernest Holt, Enoch Dixon, and Ronnie Hall became outstanding runners. Darnell Vallery and Edward Harris had remarkable seasons at quarterback behind Bubba. The year for Charlton Pollard and Coach Smith was a winning year. Everyone was happy, except Bubba, who began to think about his graduation from high school, about the future.

Mama, as she had for sixteen years, gave him 100 percent support, but he needed guidance from someone who had gone through this: he needed his brother Beaver.

Beaver, as expected, was a sensation in his rookie year at Iowa. Five touchdowns in one game. The chant in Iowa was "All the way with Willie Ray!" Beaver had spent his Christmas vacation at home, but Bubba had not decided to open up to him until he had returned to college. Besides he had changed, and the new Willie Ray, Jr., confused Bubba and the family. They hoorrahed together, played bones and worked out, yet some intangible quality of their relationship was missing.

Tody, now a member of the National Honor Society, freshman football player, and more important to him, self-assigned leader of Beaumont's get-down—volatile-temper society, challenged his oldest brother. "Beaver had turned white overnight!" Tody exclaims. "The niggah sounded like Archie Andrews and told me that his name was Ray, not Beaver. Damn." And Beaver thought Tody was "on his way to becoming a thug." Bubba no longer recognized either of his brothers; he hadn't the time. He was frantically trying to play catch-up to his new body. He continued to think like a roly-poly when everyone responded to a junior giant. They all loved each other—Georgia made sure of that—yet something else was needed to make the future make sense.

Everything seemed to be happening at once—it always does when you reach that damn growing-up stage. Charles Aaron Smith was in a whirlwind, and so were his brothers, but they were all he had—who else was there? Beaver's final remark before returning to Iowa had been "You and I have something to do. We'll break every football record ever made. Tody's unlucky—when it gets around to him, it'll all be done."

Graduation was a year away: he needed to visit his brother and see that crazy world outside of Beaumont.

He didn't pack—a gym bag was enough. Permission had been granted, so off he went, to a place he only knew from his geography books.

One thousand air miles later, when he disembarked on that cool, crisp Iowa day, he had to wipe his horn-rimmed glasses clean to make sure that what he saw was what it was. He had left black Boomahnt and had arrived in pure-white Iowa. Even the name sounded white, he thought. The only nonwhite forms were the rich soil, the ominous clouds and his reflection in the mirror of the airport weight scale. He had weighed himself, just to do something and accustom his feet to terra firma. The arrow zoomed to two hundred eight-seven pounds. Those fearful, astonished glances in his direction proved that he had not lost his height. Not one of these people knew he was a frightened teenager on his first trip abroad. He knew it was still America, but it felt like another country, and he was someone else, Othello in Venice or Gulliver perhaps. His imagination he the Iowans yelling, "There's a man on the beach!"

Back to reality, he cautiously hailed a taxi. At home were signs: COLORED CAB, WHITE TAXI, COLORED DR FOUNTAIN. No signs here, even the skycaps were whit took his best shot. No one shot back. More surprisi yellow Pontiac drove up, and the driver leaned over destination. He replied, after clearing his parche poking at the center bridge of his glasses, "Th Pleased with himself, that he had used what white voice, he climbed in, engineered his leg comfortable position, and closed the door. A roared into full gear, he saw the cap-clad dr in the mirror. He had relaxed a bit but no attentiveness. They rode a few minutes, the ing him after the airplane nap. The dri gathered courage, and asked, "Are you a b sir?" He smiled pleasantly, to assure Bubb harm. Bubba felt his fear, so he shot back, " trip was graveyard quiet.

There was a sign in front of Bubba on the seat that read, THE HAWKEYE STATE; OUR L AND OUR RIGHTS WE DEFEND. Smith prayed "our" referred to included him. What he w that his brother was as big as popcorn in t and corn grew higher here than anywhere els

—59—

Tolbert, his history teacher at Charlton Pollard, had told him so. If his brother was the corn, he could become the popper. Why not?

Journey over. Fare paid. More relaxed now, he unfolded himself out the door and said, straight-faced. "By the way, I do play basketball. My name's Bill Russell!" The driver turned. "Oh yeah, if you're Bill Russell, you sure can afford more than a quarter tip," and he sped off.

At the desk, Bubba asked for Willie Ray Smith, Jr., and the reaction of the freckle-faced, crew-cut redhead would have been the same, he imagined, if he had asked for the Pope in this heavily Roman Catholic city. The brothers Smith met and greeted each other. Ray, as he was known in Iowa, acted as if he were picking up the conversation they had been having a few weeks before; Beaver was different, though. Bubba forced his burning excitement to cool.

Bubba carefully asked his help, a little pull, so that he might join him in Iowa the next year. "My Favorite Things," that exalted sheet of sound, poured from John Coltrane's recording, immersing Willie Ray's soul. His eyes stared through Bubba. Bubba was searching for his future, and big brother Beaver was cooling out his culture. The final modulated sixth from Coltrane's saxophone brought Beav back to Iowa and Bubba. He jumped up, walked out of the room, and Bubba followed as Coltrane glided into "Everytime We Say Goodbye." They walked, without words, for minutes that seemed like days to Bubba. Beaver's hands were shoved down into his athletic cket. He had quick steps, like he thought and played. Bubba sily kept up, with his longer legs, while still acknowledging leader.

Ma's Hamburger Stand might easily have been Willie Ray's club's headquarters. He was received with a collegiate rah- The raindrops began to fall as they walked and ate the Ray rs—that's what the menu called them, after the univer- tar running back. Bubba was impressed, though only by t that these were white boys and girls who were hope-to- s of Ray. That, and only that, he had not seen before.

 stopped and sat in an alley under an awning behind all stadium. Bubba wasn't dressed for rain but the vas one of the last things on his mind.

 appeared to hear the echo of the past season's roars. d his burger, turned to his brother, and said, "I don't p here!" Bubba asked his hero for a repeat. "Go to

—— 60 ——

some other college, Bub, this is no place for you." The raindrops mixed with Bubba's tears as he left his brother and walked away.

Beaver, on his haunches, sank down and flung the hamburger wrapping away. He had done something momentous, he thought. He had just handed the baton of success to his brother. No one but he knew it, but he had only flashes of his greatness left. The high school injury in Marshall, Texas, and a few the past season at Iowa had cut his talent in half. He still had the balance, the savvy, the attitude, the flair, but those jealous, selfish good friends had done the deed. It was his brother's turn, and Bubba did not need to be in the shadow of his popularity. It was Bubba's time! The big kid had no idea why his idol had said those words to him, but it was meant to motivate him.

The only turn in Bubba's mind, those minutes, that day, was to return home. It was the deepest wound he had ever suffered. He began, however, to realize one thing: he had to decide for himself. Bubba Smith was in charge of Bubba Smith. It was his life, and no one else could make his decisions. He had gone after the answer to his future and gotten it. It was not the one he had hoped for but it had cleared up a few things.

The trip had started him up, and he whipped himself into full gear. The very night he returned home, he began preparation for his final season with his father's team. He was focused on himself for the first time. Beaver and his father had taught him everything, but until he had broken the tie between his brother and himself, he hadn't realized his own potential and talent.

The tar streets of Beaumont were soft at night, and he ran every one with his brother Tody. He was improving his time. He moved like a running back instead of a lineman. He freed himself. No longer was he a ferocious yet clumsy bear; now he was a monstrously clever eagle.

That year, the eagle smoked—that year, his last at Charlton Pollard. Before the Smiths had arrived at Beaumont, this team had been unable to chew bubblegum and run at the same time. Now, with the Coach's discipline, the new theory of teamwork was law. Georgia Smith had mothered and fed them. Some even say she had coached a few. The fans had witnessed the flights of Beaver; now they were cringing at the sound and fury of the team lead by Bubba Smith. He belonged to himself, and so did all of the team's eleven games and the district championship.

One of Charlton Pollard's victories was against their crosstown rivals, Hebert High School. A game to remember in Boomahnt. It was 2:00 PM, and already the town was lit. The cars were backed up to Eleventh Street. The radios were blasting "Hit the Road, Jack." Ray Charles was moving it. Ruby and the Romantics crooned "Our Day Will Come." Nina Simone begged "I Loves You, Porgy." The horns were blowing. The niggers were screaming at the Negroes, and the colored shook their heads and sucked their tongues. The white folks came in groups, with hard rules not to separate—move together or else. Boomahnt turn out to root for Charlton Pollard, Coach Smith, and his boys. Many followed the grain truck route to Purple Stadium and the big game. Hebert High School fans flowed from the Pear Orchard, the north side. Five hours later the football game began.

Twenty-four thousand spectators had jammed the stadium, and jammed they did. Down on the field fifty marching youngsters worked on some "Poison Ivy." They got down, right on the football field. Thelma Nixon, Charlotte Smith, and Betty Bailey, the cute trio of cheerleaders, began hopping up and down. Thighs were slashing, eyes were gleaming, and here they came, the teams onto the field. Captain Mel Farr led the Hebert Panthers in their Blue and Gold and captain Bubba Smith ran sweet in front of the Blue and White Charlton Pollard Bulldogs. Coach Smith limped behind his team and talked with his assistants. Tody moved cautiously near the front of the grandstand and wondered who, or perhaps how many, lucky ladies he would choose tonight.

The whistle filled the air, followed by the spiraling kickoff. Hebert's eleven wanted this game, it seemed. In the first quarter Hebert controlled the ball for nine minutes and thirteen seconds, whereas Charlton fumbled twice and was intercepted once. The second quarter ran the score to 20–6 in Hebert's favor.

Georgia was shook. She booked from the stands. Two hundred yards around the stadium she paced, walking off the frustration of watching her Sweetheart's team fall fourteen points behind. She played off the hoorrah's from the Hebert teachers and warned them, "She who hoorrahs last, hoorrahs best." She buoyed the hopes of every Charlton Pollard fan, no matter the race. "Keep the faith!" "We're number 1!" She stood along the path by which the team would re-enter for the second half. A roar of hope welcomed them, and she yelled the loudest.

She kissed her Sweetheart good luck. Coach Smith, warily looking for any note in her hands, relaxed when she sheepishly showed him her empty palms. He smiled his Doll smile, and continued to the bench.

"You can win—keep trying," she cooed to her son Bubba. "Mother, I promised Daddy in the locker room that we will win this game for him. Coach said to make three touchdowns and stop them, and that's what we're going to do. I'm personally going to grab everybody, sort them, toss, 'til I find the one with the ball, and keep him." He kissed his mother, yanked on his helmet, and trotted away.

It seemed warmer than it had been at game team. The fans seemed louder; there was no doubt they were drunker. No one on the team was allowed anything stronger than Coca-Cola, but they were higher than the flagpole that second half.

Bubba noticed in the first plays that whenever Hebert's quarterback, Mel Farr, signaled for a screen pass, his fullback and halfback shifted position. He told his fellow defenders in the huddle that he would holler the word Sam when it was coming. Two plays later it happened: "Sam" Mel threw a screen pass and Howard Biggs intercepted and ran forty-five yards for a Charlton touchdown.

Hebert on the next series of plays took the ball to the Pollard three-yard line. It was first down and goal. Four times they tried, and Harvey Henry, Kelly Vallery, Harvey Dixon, Robert Chambers, Jefferson Womack, Edward Williams, and their captain held them scoreless. The biology teacher screamed so loud that three windows broke in the biology department, and you know who fainted.

The Coach's team had followed his halftime command, winning 24–20. Not a point was scored against Bubba's defensive unit. It was the final game, and they had won them all.

Only four colleges though had offered scholarships to Bubba, ninety-seven less than had pursued his illustrious brother, and Charles Aaron forgot what everyone in the streets knew, even when all they played was touch football—the only popular positions were wide receiver, running back, and quarterback. No one ever thought of linemen.

Moses saw him in the locker room. He was last to leave the stadium. Bubba was a moody young man—a sudden shift and the world would have to wait a couple of days for any response. Moses, though, seemed unworldly, and he walked through the wall of gloom.

They sat there, two African-Americans, one having seen it all, the other about to. Words were not important; it was a spiritual time.

The all-star basketball and football games were sponsored by Houston's Negro newspaper, the *Forward Times*. Lloyd Wells, photographer, sports editor, con man, and chief hoorrah niggah of Texas, was the host. It was a house-of-shock niggah weekend in Houston. July 1963: the official reasons were to show off the Negro talent of Texas and make a few dollars for charity; but if you couldn't hang—don't come. You had to protect yourself with your attitude, your mouth, and your talent.

The night before the basketball game was the test—it was shit-talking night at the Groovy Grill. The women, ladies, bitches, and girls were there; the men, dudes, pimps, and cats were there; the music was cooking. James Brown was frying, and it was hot. The temperature outside was a cool 98 degrees; inside, forget it. Black, brown, hazel, green, gold, every sparkling eye glistened with hope, desire, and joy. And bodies, oh yes, the soft curves, hips, breasts, legs, all of it was alive. All the real reasons for playing this weekend, besides the scouts, were there.

It was a six-feet nine-inch papersack-colored niggah named David Latin who was sharing the spotlight with Bubba. Latin was a lover and was loud and proud. "I'm gonna suck your guts outta yo body" was his opener for the giggling girlies. He stood like a giant, his hand outstretched, and his eyes searching the ceiling. "Ahm gonna barbecue yo nuts tamorrah night, Bubber Smith." Ooowee, said the lovely ladies.

Smith was there, holding up a wall and watching David hold court. A faint smile moved the ends of his mouth. He nodded his head, put the index finger up to the middle of his glasses, and simply said "Ahm gonna denut you, Latin!" A long finger pointed toward his target. "I'll see you up in barbecue country. We'll see who'll burn, he said and walked slowly out. Mmmh, said the females, wishing they were on his arm.

It went on into the night, after the athletes under curfew had left. The pregame promotion had accomplished its objective, and the paying customers were choosing their own stars for the evening.

The game became an explosion of fury. If the other basketball players on either the East or West were fired up, Bubba and David were a furnace. David Latin, although a better basketball player, met his match for a moment. Bubba stuffed, snatched, and slapped until he fouled out with four minutes twenty seconds remaining. Coach Willie Ray's East team lost, and his son sank into himself. He was not accustomed to losing anything. But when he began pouting like a spoiled brat, his father gave him some advice. "You don't play anything well mad. You must call the football game tomorrow with players who you've never played with. The better team won tonight, but tomorrow is your time. I'm depending on you to be what you've worked so hard to be." Bubba went straight home. No Groovy Grill. No hoorrah. Just rest.

The football game was another story. Eight hours sleep, a healthy lecture, and he felt like a prince.

A Houston summer day in Jeppensen Stadium. The field temperature was higher than the alcoholic content of the Thunderbird, Peppermint Twist, and Silver Satin wine soaked up by the faithful. The game was called both offensively and defensively by Bubba. Each play was described fully in the huddle. His fellow teammates included Mel Farr, Gene Washington, and Ernest Holt. Although the score failed to show it, by half time Bubba and his team knew they had won. Complete control of the adversary and the teamwork among so-called strangers made it easy.

Bubba could relax a little and rediscover a personal enemy. He noticed him only after being completely confident of the outcome of the game. He went so far as to re-introduce himself at half time to Doug Smith. At one hundred eighty pounds, six-foot three-inch Doug played for Aldine High School. Charlton Pollard and Aldine had played one month before the All-Star game, and he was remembered well by Bubba—he had caught Bubba unprotected. Defending against an Aldine blitz, Bubba, number 55 had snatched two of the invading lineman. He held them with his massive arms, leaving his face wide open, an invitation that this same Douglas Smith, Jr., had accepted, joyously. His forearm had caused forty-six stitches inside and three outside of Bubba's bottom lip. The numerals on Bubba's jersey were bathed in blood. Bubba dreamed about a man for the first time, probably the last time, of his teen-age life that night.

And here he was, smiling Douglas, relaxed after Bubba's handshake and pleasant greeting. It was the third quarter, and Bubba's signal in the huddle called for him to line up directly in front of the kid from Aldine. The ball was snapped, and so was

Douglas. His mother had difficulty recognizing her child that afternoon in the hospital. It was never his style to plan the destruction of another player, but he knew he had to teach the child a lesson. He became Professor Smith that day. Douglas lived to play again but his style was professional after that—he never took advantage of anyone.

The East won the game, 24–6. Ernest Holt, running back, and Bubba were awarded co-MVP awards. After the game a man named Moses drove his moving truck away from the stadium. Those who saw him said he was smiling and singing "Let My People Go."

The college scouts awakened after his all-star performance, and they offered him the other world. Back home in Beaumont the telegram boy was so busy he tipped Bubba. The news was ticking for one brother, but Beaver had been injured again and had missed being chosen All-American.

Mel Farr, a fine quarterback and, more important than that, a running buddy of Bubba's, had chosen UCLA. When he arrived in the land of Hollywood, he began to dream and dreamed Bubba was on his team. He told Coach Tom Protho about this Texas lineman and advised him to grab Bubba quick. They, Protho and Bubba, talked long-distance, and Bubba heard insecurity in his voice. Protho even asked Bubba to spend a year at Santa Monica College before joining UCLA, to get him ready, he said. Bubba passed.

In 1956 Hugh "Duffy" Daugherty was named college football coach of the year. Seven years later the coach of Michigan State University arrived in Beaumont, Texas. His objective: to sign Bubba Smith to a scholarship. Smith had not signed his national letter of intent naming the college of his choice. He was fair game.

Daugherty arrived, and Coach Smith and Bubba met him at the airport. After the usual nice-to-see-you, Bubba suggested to the coach from Michigan that he should, if at all possible, watch his grammar when he got to the Smith home, because awaiting him was the most valuable player of them all, Georgia Smith. The lady fascinated Bubba almost as much as football, sometimes more. Mama stretched his intellect while Coach flexed his talent.

They arrived at Port Street, Daugherty was welcomed, and in a matter of fifteen food-filled minutes, Mama had Bubba shaking like a motorboat engine. His problem: he was trying to be cool. If he hadn't been trying, he would have been roaring out of control on the living room floor.

Georgia's technique was awesome. Imagine you are a celebrated white coach, and wherever you go, it's always red carpet time. If you have chosen a young man for your school, it may mean success, fame, the works for him. You are next to being a king, but in Boomahnt you are close to funny farm time. You have just spoken to a Negro family with a talented son, and the lady of the house corrects your syntax and repeats your words back to you in the Queen's English. After she has made you appear as if you ought to consider returning to kindergarten, she then requests that her son be given a white roommate who doesn't play football. All of this before you have officially requested his presence at your school.

Daugherty was speechless, but like a good administrator he knew what he needed. He did not go away empty-handed. Bubba promised to try Michigan State, not only because he was interested but because his father advised him to, and the Coach was always right. Daugherty departed Beaumont, unexpectedly dizzy but successful.

The notorious crab syndrome now reached Bubba, although it didn't hurt Bubba as much as it had Beaver. The elated teenager, feeling good about his new plans, was cleaning out his Charlton Pollard locker. He had forgotten a love letter and a Bible, and he was sure he would need both in faraway Michigan. The love letter was a scorcher from Linda Williams, his second hope-to-die love. It would be cold in the North, and he would need some kind of heat. The Bible was a gift from Moses, given to him on his graduation day.

He was interrupted by an assistant coach. "You'll never make it up there with the big boys." Every sound he made seemed shoved through a strainer. "Those corn-fed white boys will lynch your fat ass without your pappy."

Bubba just turned and looked at the assistant coach and whispered, "You'll regret those words." He wanted to say *nigger*, but he was taught to respect his elders.

Nineteen sixty-three—a memorable year for Americans, for both good and evil. A sniper ambushed and killed Medgar Evers in Jackson, Mississippi. The good was the March on Washington, a march by half a million loving hearts, all praying for civil rights for all Americans. The highlight of the demonstration was an address by the Rev. Dr. Martin Luther

King, Jr. He was cheered wildly when he said: "I have a dream that one day on the red hills of Georgia the sons of former slaves and the sons of former slaveowners will be able to sit down together at the table of brotherhood. I have a dream. . . . I have a dream that my four little children will one day live in a nation where they will be judged not by the color of their skin but by the content of their character."

Willie Ray, Sr., and Georgia Smith prayed for the same dream twelve hundred miles away in Beaumont, Texas. The three Smith sons were moving on up. Willie Ray, Jr., transferred to Kansas; Tody graduated to Charlton Pollard High School; and big Bub was on his way to a foreign land called Michigan. The word *Michigan,* from *micigama,* means large water, and Bubba Smith, now weighing three hundred ten pounds and standing six feet eight inches tall, prayed he could float with the big boys.

Love, on the romance side, was also in his thoughts when he bade goodbye to his family and the angelic Moses. He leaned back in his first first-class jet plane seat and daydreamed about carmel-colored, curvaceous, calf-eyed Linda. He had promised his bursting eighteen-year-old self to her with only one qualification—time. "Give me enough time to find out how good I am in college football," he asked. She agreed, and they made their bond.

Magazines were offered to him, magazines bearing images of a smiling President Kennedy, a frowning President Kennedy, President Kennedy on his sailboat, and President Kennedy playing tag football on the White House lawn with his brothers Bobby and Ted. Bubba smiled and thought of Beaver, Tody, and himself playing football anywhere, especially on the White House lawn. His imagination wandered, seeing President Beaver weaving his way through Congress on his way to give his State of the Universe speech—Ol' Beav' was in touch with the beyond—and Secretary of State Coach Smith charming the hell out of the Queen of England. Of course Georgia would be the Secretary of the Treasury. The country's budget would have no problem with Georgia in charge of the bucks. Tody of course would be both the Secretary of War as well as the ambassador to wherever the pretty ladies were. Bubba laughed out loud at the sight of the Smith men in tails, but quickly remembering where he was, he looked both left and right to see if anyone had seen him fantasizing. The coast was clear and very white, he thought.

"Damn," he said out loud. "Damn, ever since that night in Orange when I saw that Negro branded!" He removed his shoes and gently massaged his in-grown toenail, those forever aching toes. "Yes, it started then—the question, the one that invaded my soul. Why do white people hate me?"

It was a good question, one that most thinking Negroes ask sooner or later, a question without an answer. But Bubba wanted one now, before he arrived in that other place—college.

CHAPTER 5

I Had Watched *The Untouchables* on Television, so I Knew about Italians, but What the Hell Was a Jew?

HE WAS NOW A SEASONED TRAVELER, having flown to Iowa. Refusing any alcoholic beverages, he remained loyal to Coca-Cola on the rocks and settled down in his seat for the flight.

He noticed a man looking his way. As their eyes met, the man ducked into his book. He looked a second time, and there was no response. His gaze fell to the book, and the jacket read *A Fire Next Time* by James Baldwin. The name was familiar, a Negro writer out of New York, but the title intrigued him, and so did the fact that a white man was reading a book written by a Negro. He presumed the story was about Negroes and wondered what the man was learning about his people. One thing was certain, Bubba didn't know a thing about the reader.

He had known only one white person in his life, Butch Hoffer, the owner of the clothing store in Beaumont. Bald, chubby Butch was always pleasant, always making corny remarks that Bubba never understood, and the remark was always followed by a nervous but full laugh. Mr. Hoffer had treated him well, but Mama always had all the bills paid on time. Why wouldn't a merchant be nice to me, he thought. It was only a business relationship, not a real friendship. Everything he had heard, read, or saw made it quite clear to Bubba that there was a difference between him and them.

If the man had looked at him, if the man and he had talked, what would they say? Would he be asked if he were a basketball player? What else would a tall Negro be? That guy, of course, had to be a businessman. What else could he be?

The two first-class travelers never made contact, remaining strangers. Perhaps next time, when Bubba was a successful athlete, successful, known everywhere—when he was a star, everyone would talk to a star. He drifted off to sleep, dreaming of his future, never doubting his talent, only wondering how he would handle the pressure.

He awoke to the sweet voice over the loudspeaker. He straightened himself and looked at the harried stewardess. He remembered that she was forbidden territory. One of the most talented football players on the Michigan State graduating team had warned him about the rules. "Never be caught with a white female at school." Direct from the horse's mouth—Herb Adderly had just been drafted number 1 by the Green Bay Packers, but he had paid the price for his curiosity in his final season at school, the same school Bubba was arriving at. Adderly played only sixty minutes the entire football season because he had been *seen* with a white woman.

Bub couldn't have been more grateful for the warning. It surely wasn't the first time that Bubba had heard the rule—Negroes had been lynched for merely looking at a white female. What did the White Queen possess? Magic or maybe a precious stone, a gem set in her heart. Bubba wondered. It had to be something, or why would men kill and be killed for her? The opening airliner door jolted him back to reality. Lansing, Michigan's capital, home of the Michigan State Spartans, and perhaps the answer to all of his questions.

The same sun, the same day, the same Bubba from Beaumont, Texas. An August day in Michigan. Assistant coach Danny Boisture shoved his hand into Bubba's, and he was welcomed. They talked sports trivia while Boisture drove, giving the rookie the tourist route. Most of the conversation concerned football, a world that both understood.

Back on the range in the Lone Star State. The backyard of the Vice President of the United States. In Beaumont, there were some puffs of dust seen and ferocious snorts heard from the football field. El Toro had sauntered onto center stage, Charlton Pollard. Crepe had been hung on the doors and windows of the Dew Drop Inn as well as Lode's Pool Hall. Tody Smith, aka

Baby Huey, aka Lawrence Edward, was not coming to high school, he was here. All six feet six inches and two hundred fifty pounds, with style, sat with the other rookies in front of Coach Smith.

Tody had heard the opening-day speech a dozen times, but aware of his being the heir to a legend, he listened attentively. He knew of the problems both his brothers had suffered, of the envy of others; he had his own way of handling any waves. Tody, unlike his brothers, both squares, had grown up in Beaumont in bad-ass country. Tody had hung with the street folk, and their law was his—Get them before they get you. Add flair to this theory and an honor-student brightness, and you have the reason Coach Smith read the riot act twice that opening day.

Beaver, the first born, had been closest to their father. Bubba was the solid one, the dependable loving son. Tody was the carbon copy of the Coach when he was a teenager, the adventurous, lover boy Doll. Father Smith enjoyed every minute with his son. Coach Smith thanked God that Tody was on his team, but his hand stayed on his board of education in case.

Bubba was the eagle, Tody the bull, and big brother Willie Ray, Jr., was the stallion, the finest racehorse anyone had seen in Texas, or Iowa.

In Michigan freshman collegian Charles Aaron Smith, rookie Spartan, was introduced to his campus. Or was it Peter Prep or Irving Ivy? The eighteen-year-old mountain appeared his first day in fashions straight out of *Ozzie and Harriet.* He was in style for the campus. A houndstooth sports jacket, khaki slacks with a razor-edge crease, matching socks, and penny loafers. Mama had starched his white shirts, and adorning this cardboard blouse, he wore a pencil-thin necktie. The perfect picture of a college kid in a boy-next-door movie about white America. The only problem, if it was a problem, was that the young man was chestnut brown, weighed three hundred pounds plus, was nearing seven feet, wore a size 52XL jacket and size fourteen shoes, and was the only person who looked quite like this on a campus filled with forty thousand Americans. If a Negro from a stereotypical ghetto in America had witnessed this costume, they would have dropped to their knees in hysterical laughter. Let's face it—the freshman was a definite square, with horn-rimmed glasses and a *Quo Vadis* haircut.

The square giant walked through the administration doors,

on a humid Michigan morning, filled to overflowing with expectation. The campus thrilled his eye. Every inch of grass was manicured beyond his wildest imagination. The scents were different, and they awakened his mind. The student body had a month before checking-in. The only students on campus were athletes.

He shook the hands of the administrators, who were awed by his size, but who were reassured by his manner of dress. At least he looked civilized, and his home training, saying *yes, ma'am* and *no, sir,* made some even smile.

Some were smiling about the money he would bring to the school. They could see the new buildings being erected by the profit from his talent. Some were genuinely good people. A good person handed Bubba a manila envelope filled with facts about his new home. One paper described his job. He unfolded this sheet of paper, adjusted his glasses, leaned against the mahogany tabletop, and perused his schedule. Bubba hadn't given anything about Michigan State, except football, his attention. This was just a ritual, he thought, one of the many that collegiates, like himself, had to endure.

Besides his corn shucking at Nanny Lonie's in Nacogdoches and waxing the floors in his home, this would be his maiden voyage into work. Certainly sports and sex were pleasure and shouldn't be counted. Work meant 9:00 to 5:00 and all the rest. Twice he removed his prescription glasses and cleaned them furiously with one of the starched handkerchiefs that his mother had given him. He was giddy from what he had read—there must have been a mistake. An eight-hour construction job, tarring the ancient roofs of the University. They couldn't be serious, thought the freshman. There was little doubt that he was being asked to perform an act of labor.

Before doing anything, even complaining, he remembered the magic words of his grandmother: "It's nice to be nice." Remembering the phrase, the word *sheeet* kept interfering with his thoughts.

Hunger, a sudden obscene growling engulfed his mammoth frame, and he moved to stanch it. To the commissary he went. As soon as he opened the doors, he knew he would be disappointed. Mama Smith had thoroughly spoiled him, even with the aromas from her kitchen. These smells were bland, even boring. He looked for a Negro in the open kitchen; none could be seen. He asked to make sure, perhaps they were hidden in the back room somewhere. The words that spilled from the thin-lipped woman who stood, pleasant and warm, behind the counter shook him. "I'm sorry we have no grits!" No Grits! He pined for them now more than when he had asked for them. Smith had a grits attack, and he hurried out into the vastness of the campus and felt more alone then he had since his arrival.

By the following week he had met a few Negro athletes and a few workers on the campus who knew where grits could be found. Problem 1 had been solved.

The freshman team meeting was scheduled for that Wednesday, and he appeared, attempting to look as relaxed and as secure as possible. They met in a dormitory classroom. He wore a sweater over a sportshirt, slacks, and the brand-new Converse sneakers his mother had given him for college. He wore them because he was to report after his meeting to his job for the first time. He had thought about it, weighing both pro and con, and had decided to give it a try. You never know—it may be a foreman's job.

Here he was, though, in his first team meeting. He noticed that eleven of his teammates were Negro, and that made him sigh, a deep sigh of relief. Two were home boys and friends, Gene Washington and Jess Phillips. They had arrived late, and they welcomed each other.

A five-foot three-inch gentleman wearing horn-rimmed spectacles walked into the crowded room. He was announced by his assistant as freshman coach Burt Smith. Another Smith with glasses. Bubba said to himself, if you have patience, it'll all work out. A smile appeared on his face.

Coach Burt Smith asked each of the players to stand, give his name, school, and major achievements, in alphabetical order. Their credentials would have challenged a five-star general's, thought Bubba, who was happy he was an S, an S far down the line on this thirty-five man roster. Everyone seemed to be an All-American, suggesting to Bubba that not only were they excellent athletes but that they must have come from either white or integrated schools and cities. Not one Negro high school, at least in Texas, had been given All-American status. Thank God he came at the end, or he would have given his name and school and sat down.

It was his turn. He eased his six feet eight inches slowly out of the uncomfortable wooden class chair and lowered his voice to sound like the then-popular Negro singer Billy Eckstine. "Bubba Smith, all-state two years." He glowered at the others, paused, and placed himself back in his seat. He knew how to play the competition game, and he performed his opening act successfully. The hoorrah session began. Pat Gallinor, a white athlete from Detroit, and Charles 'Mad Dog' Thornhill, a black from Virginia, got down. "I can do one-hundred pushups," one said. "I can do one-hundred on my fingertips," the other shot back. "I can do one-hundred with a two-hundred-pound man on my back, on my thumbs." It went on like that until the atmosphere became a little easier to breathe. Mad Dog, sometimes called the Greek God, because of his Mr. Universe–muscled body, delighted them all with his antics, and Bubba became his hoorrah partner. Bubba's technique had grown sophisticated after years of living with hoorrah giants. He would use the slick, signifying method, while Thornhill was the loud put-down artist.

Another Negro, George Webster from Anderson, South Carolina, began talking after the meeting ended, and they seemed to enjoy each other's spirit. Bubba was amazed by George's perfect teeth and his classic look. He still couldn't lose that roly-poly other self in his mind, and not until he discovered long distance spitting did he like his Smith gap, the space between his two front teeth—everyone in the family had it.

It was work time, and he reported faithfully on the dot. When he reminded them why he was at Michigan State, they handed him a rake and pointed to a truck. Bubba tried it, he did. Sixty minutes of raking that smelly stuff, which splattered on his Converses, his sparkling white sneakers. The foreman noticed his displeasure and switched him to what he thought might please a young man of his size. The job was the jackhammer, and it shook Bubba senseless. It was called a blue brute, and it was.

Thirty minutes later he was back in his temporary room at the Kappa house, shaking and frantically cleaning his Converses. His phone rang. It was Tennessee—the football coach was asking, "How ya doing big fella?" Bubba was pleasantly surprised. "How did you find me?" "We have our ways," laughed the voice.

He wanted a last crack at Smith and offered a ticket to the college all-star game in Chicago, where they would confer with him in a neighboring motel. Bubba still had not signed his national letter of intent; he remained fair game. He heard the hunger in the coach's voice, and he cleverly sneaked in, "I did want to go home." The Tennessee coach fielded the words passionately, assuring the freshman, "Don't worry about it, mah son!"

Two tickets awaited the veteran traveler at the Lansing

airport. Bubba packed and reviewed his alternatives at the counter. He began patting his thigh, a sure sign of nervousness. Although tarring roofs was a pain in the behind, and the blue brute had pained him everywhere else, what would happen when he returned to Beaumont? That pain might be magnified a thousandfold. He was and always would be Coach and Georgia Smith's son. And Coach would always have that board of education in his back pocket. He would never get too old for that, of that he was certain. Yet he boarded the flight to Beaumont.

The knock at the family door was weak, to say the very least. Georgia asked, "Who is it?" at least five times before her son would reply. "What are you doing in Beaumont?" was the hard one. The answer to that flowed through the gap in Bubba's front teeth without passing through his brain. "They gave me all this menial labor," he said and exaggerated the details of his work. He went on and on, until his mother had had enough. "And that's why you're not in college?" she asked. Mama folded her arms and frowned at her son. "I can't believe that my son, your daddy's child, is a quitter." The word rocked him—his ears had never, ever, heard it directed at their owner. He cleared his throat, leaned down, picked up his luggage, straightened, kissed his mother, turned, and walked away. Not a word passed between them after *quitter*. A tear glided down Mama's cheek as she silently watched her young man leave.

Of course it was impossible for him to sneak back to his room without being seen by anyone in Lansing or on the Michigan State campus, but that was the official word the next morning. Not a soul had missed him. Marlon Brando would have been proud of the quality of the acting on campus.

One of the better thespians was freshman coach Smith, who watched him sign his letter of intent to play with the Spartans, in exchange for a new job and a concerted effort in the commissary to find grits, whatever they were.

Freshman squad practice the following day. Bubba was fired up for his first practice scrimmage and wanted to show Jerry Rust everything that he had. He made a complete fool of Mr. Rust that day and gained a little respect from some of his teammates.

Back to his room he went, feeling as though he might even stay at Michigan, at least for a while, and flopped himself on the top deck of the doubledeck bed. One minute later he was dreaming the good dreams of a college freshman fifteen hundred miles away from lovely Linda in Beaumont.

He slept the sleep of angels the next month practicing hard everyday. He began to feel as he thought he would when he had first heard of college. He was a lonely giant, though awaiting his roomie; the name Clyde Norman was presented to him by the dean of men one day. Clyde would be his roommate, and Bubba would begin to learn about them, those other Americans who weren't blessed with color but owned everything, including his sport.

After a good healthy workout that drizzling day in September, he decided to take a nap. Stripped naked, he climbed to his royal perch on the top deck and dozed. Someone should have given some warning, but there came Clyde, five-foot one-inch Clyde from the Upper Peninsula of Michigan. In he walked, with Mama and Papa Norman bringing up the rear. Bubba heard the commotion, felt their presence, opened his eyes, and playfully leaped from the top deck to the ground. Undressed for his nap, he wasn't fully aware of the Norman family until it was too late. Now, a gingerbread giant leaping down from the sky would give most anyone at least a minor surprise; But for a four-foot eleven-inch forty-year-old lady and a five-foot forty-year-old man and their son it was the monster-movie shock of their lives. So unnerved were the Normans of Michigan, they passed out like falling dominoes, one on top of another, leaving a surprised Bubba alone with three white people resting comfortably at his feet.

Dressed in his favorite outfit—walking shorts and tee shirt-he sat awaiting their awakening. Recovered, each professed embarrasment and communication began, sort of. Bubba is a charmer, though—when the situation calls it—and the Normans left their son behind, in the same room with him, alone.

For the next month itwas a hi-how-are-you relationship. Freshman Smith had other problems, such as never being asked to practice with the varsity football team like some of his other teammates were. Clyde would just have to come around on his own. Everytime Bubba walked into the room, timid Norman would stuff his face into a book. Either he was a twenty-four-hour brain, or he didn't want to understand his roomie. One thing was excellent—the young man was trained for housekeeping. The Smith-Norman room stayed spic-and-span, delighting No-labor Smith. It wasn't however, accomplishing the objective:

Bubba was not finding out how a white person thought; one crisp Michigan day the melting process of an icy relationship began with the kind of subtle approach that would become a Bubba trademark. "Do you ever do or say anything, Clyde?" A look of real consternation was stamped plainly on his huge face as he spoke.

Clyde bit the bullet and explained himself. He was depressed, was Clyde, down in a melancholia attributable to a misunderstanding with a member of the female sex. In Bubba's words, "Some woman had messed with Clyde's head!"

Ah, it wasn't because Bubba was a Negro or anything of the like; it was only a broad. Smith could relate to that, having a similar problem with his Linda, and not one possibility on campus. There were forty-seven Negro females on campus. None qualified.

Bubba would teach Norman how to ease the pain through music. Clyde was introduced, that languid Lansing afternoon, to Little Anthony and the Imperials, Little Stevie Wonder, and the Supremes. Mr. Norman had dealt with Eddie Fisher, Andy Williams, and (a one and a two and a) Lawrence Welk. Bubba was positive that his education should begin at the absolute beginning. Bubba's records demonstrated how to use the heartbroken lyrics and the throbbing heartbeat of the orchestration to overwhelm any pain in life. The curing of the blues was easy with music, if only because you could play a record over and over again until you were cleansed. Clyde was delighted.

The other problem disturbing Norman was his father's sickness. In Bubba's efforts to win him over, Bubba transformed Clyde's fear for his daddy's life into the possibility of his own father becoming sick. Feeling the same pain, they cried together, and a friendship began.

Clyde was cured and the following month Bubba became sure of his talent as a psychologist. He was about to enter their room when he overheard Clyde talking to a few of his white classmates. All of the young people were awed by Bubba's size.

They had never known a Negro before, much less a giant football player from Texas. Remaining at the door, Bubba overheard Clyde explaining to his friends about his Main Man Bubba. "He's my ace! Bub cleans up on Monday, Wednesday, and Friday, and I do it the rest of the week. Ol' Bubba even lends me his car whenever I ask for it. Bubba is a down dude!" Bubba couldn't contain himself after the Norman conversation and walked in humming. Bubba apologized for disturbing the group and for not having the room cleaned, today being Wednesday. With that he threw his car keys to Clyde, saying "I filled the tank and had it washed. Anything else you need?" The group looked at each other, shook their heads, and looked at their friend Clyde as if he were the luckiest guy in all of Michigan. Norman ordered pizza that night and paid for it, and they listened to their favorite records featuring their favorite entertainers, Little Anthonly and the Imperials, Stevie Wonder, and the Supremes.

Back at the practice field, and Burt Smith, the freshman coach, who was becoming a true friend as well as an honest coach, had a problem placing number 55. If he played center, the quarterback had a hard time seeing his receivers. Bubba played offensive tackle, then tight end. In his frustration he beat up on the freshman once, running through, over, and beyond six defending linemen for an intercepted pass and a touchdown.

He wasn't needed, he felt, until he joined the varsity squad, and he really didn't care to waste his talent hurting his teammates. He needed time in his avocation, discovering white people, but he was thrown a curve, when he asked about one of the white people and was informed that the student was not white but a Jew. "A what?" Bubba asked. He had heard the word, but he really never knew what it meant, nor had he ever met one. "How can you tell whether he's a Jew or one of you?" His question was simple but a bit unusual, causing the astonished WASP student to fumble a quick reply. "Look at his nose," he said and hurried away, never looking back.

Bubba Smith, mammoth Charles Aaron Smith, walked around a campus filled with forty-four thousand young people, of whom only two hundred ninety were black; the rest were fair game for the inquisitive young man from Beaumont. When he wasn't checking noses, he was reading. He had heard of Italians from the television series *The Untouchables*, but this new creation, a Jew, piqued his curiosity.

As soon as the whistle ending practice blew, number 55 would be heading to the university library to learn more. To his amazement, Jewish and African-American histories were a lot alike. They suffered, check. They were a minority, check. They were not allowed equal privileges, check. They were forced to live in separate sections called ghettos, check. They were persecuted, check. During World War II, Adolph Hitler had killed millions of Jews. Damn. Adolph was a low life. So was Lee Harvey Oswald.

His latest avocation was cancelled for a while, and so was everyone else's. The Big Ten championship, Michigan State vs. Illinois was postponed. John Fitzgerald Kennedy, thirty-fifth

President of the United States, had been shot and fatally wounded in Dallas.

Bubba had not worshiped the new president like many other Americans; he had been too involved in football. Sensitive, though, his heart went out to his devastated new friends—some cried openly—yet Bubba wondered what their reaction would have been to the death of the man he had seen branded and butchered in Orange.

The leaves were now a ruby rust or burnt orange, Lake Michigan floated icebergs, and the temperature hovered between 20 or 30 degrees. The football team had won six and lost three but Illinois had won the Big Ten, and Bubba Smith would have his chance at the varsity squad.

He asked his best friend, George Webster, who lived across the hall, "When is it going to snow?" George who seemed to know everything, with his perfect self (his perfect speech, his perfect teeth, his perfect face) replied, "How the hell should I know? I'm from South Carolina." Bubba had never witnessed snow. "I'd seen the stuff on television, but I wanted to feel it." As though he were a magician Bubba awoke the next morning to a winter wonderland—four feet of wonder.

Clyde, who still had female problems and a huge record collection, looked at his hero as one would look at a mental patient. Master Norman had grown up in Michigan and had learned to hate snow—the last freak on his mind would be one who danced around a room in his underwear celebrating the wet stuff. But with a forget-you-snob-Norman note in his manner and a child's dream in his heart, Bubba bounced his mammoth self out into it. Everyone in the hallways and outside in the snow either joined in his spirit or asked, "What's wrong with that big niggah?" Of course anyone asking the question, said it to themselves. Bub, though, had to act like all Americans—he made a snowman and tossed snowballs. An hour later, Smith's work of art stood solidly in front of the northeast windows of Wonders Hall. A problem had arisen, a heartbreaking one. The tall Texan had come to realize that the white stuff was wet, very wet, and cold, very, very cold. In fact, Charles Aaron was freezing his ass off, and disenchantment set in like a sacked quarterback. It would be his final contact with the shit.

When the shit had melted and spring had sprung, he was back to his true love, football. The freshmen had a spring practice game. One team wore green jerseys, the other white.

Bubba could have worn either, he was into the other team's line so often. He had a great game—the student body took notice, but no one who mattered did. A completely frustrating first year. "They're teaching stuff I mastered in the tenth grade," he muttered to George. Webster only nodded and kept playing. Webster had a ton of talent, but his training was nowhere near as thorough as Bubba's; whose was?

If they let you play with the varsity, it's a recognition of your talent, thought Smith. Everyone else seemed to get the opportunity. One practice game saw Bubba receive a short pass and run sixty-seven yards for a touchdown. Still he wasn't called up to the main team's practices.

He remained depressed that year, playing basketball to stay in shape and sharpening his education. His struggle with classwork continued: "I couldn't relate it to life and football." Only the anatomy class taught him something he could use in a sport of his choice.

Two subjects remained of interest: romance and white and Jewish people. He had made a decision about the ladies—Linda had burned him—they were fun and sport, nothing else. No decision was made about the foreigners, those without color in their skin. Everything he read about them led to money. "I wanted to learn the difference between big money and small money. All of the coins were in the hands of the Steins, Steins or Bergs. I wondered how Bubbaberg or Smithstein would sound."

It was an odd college life, to say the very least. Pigskin was the reason he was here, but his own skin and that of others consumed his thoughts. To his amazement, he and all the other Negroes were now referred to as blacks. A congressman from New York, Adam Clayton Powell, had said "Black is beautiful," and soon Stokeley Carmichael called for Black Power. If anyone in Boomanht, Texas, had called Bubba black anytime before the change, their life would have been in deep jeopardy.

All this political and racial stuff, though, was getting in the way of his major interest, his career. He found himself alone a great deal. His roommate, had flunked out of Michigan State and had taken his soulful collection of long-playing records and left his girlfriend's picture behind. George Webster moved in—so much for living with white folks.

The members of the 1962 Spartan team who hadn't been drafted into the professional world of football were employed at the school as graduate assistants. These assistants were the brains of the freshman team, along with Burt Smith. A wonderful man, Burt possessed a fine football mind, yet neither he nor his assistants could discover which position suited Bubba. Bubba played well, but the team balance was off, and no one knew how to correct the problem. Bubba began to work out by himself, strengthening his weaknesses and refining his strengths.

Compare it to having a rotten week and awaking Monday morning refreshed and prepared for a new and better week, and someone cancels the week.

Now a sophomore, Smith had reported to the team meeting early, and what did his glasses magnify but the depth chart, an inked list of names, positions, and teams. Number 95, SMITH, was on the third team, and for the life of him he could not understand why. He left the meeting and drove aimlessly for an hour. He just had to drive. Returning, he screeched to a stop, slammed the door and felt a need for food, anything to fill the emptiness of not being wanted.

At the commissary he ordered the only items his Boomanht tastebuds could relate to—chili and a grilled ham and cheese sandwich—and waited to be served. Waiting, his slender fingers tapped out Morse Code on his leg, and his body shifted its three hundred ten pounds from left to right. He smiled at his fellow students, who were just beginning to like his being one of them, and waited. He reached over the counter with one of his tree-trunk arms, and "I grabbed me a whole handful of what I thought was salteen crackers. I snatched a bunch of those bad boys and took a bite. It tasted like paper. I spit it out and said to the clerk, 'What is this stuff?'" The commissary had discovered, along with Bubba, that there were Jewish students on campus. The crackers were square and corrugated—matzo—unleavened bread. The only passover on Bubba's mind, though, was his football team's over him. He returned the remaining paper still in his hand, accepted his order, ate, and booked.

Suiting up for the first two games of the college season to sit on the bench in front of all those people pained Bubba. He was always a team player, a good player, better than many of those who were starting, and he was unhappy. He had not been given a righteous chance to compete. Then his number was called. He had attended the team meeting almost by reflex, but his attitude changed: "Number 95, first team, tight end against USC." "Damn, they want me to play," he shouted.

When he walked out that Saturday morning onto the field of Spartan Stadium, he felt as though he belonged, for the very first time, to Michigan State. He had realized why he had been chosen after seeing the USC game films. The team from California was rated number 2 in the nation, and their major touchdown maker was the power sweep, a sweep aimed at Bubba Smith.

The Texas kid was as ready as anyone on the Michigan turf that day, stopping everyone and every style of play that came his way. He sacked, cracked, and slapped his way to victory.

After the game electricity ran through the Michigan locker room. All of his friends, Gene Washington, George Webster, and Mad Dog Thornhill, were beating Bubba with congratulations. An assistant coach, Cal Stoll, went as far as to hug him with appreciation. Bubba dodged the kiss, but felt as though he were on top of the world. The eagle was taking his first solo flights in the college world. He called his mother to tell her the news.

Number 95 played off and on the rest of the season. "Duffy Daugherty didn't really trust me one hundred percent." The Michigan State students, during that miserable season, did not trust Duffy at all, and every chance they got, they hung him in effigy. A form the size and shape of the coach was strung up in every public place on the campus, and one dangled from Bubba Smith's window. What comes around, goes around.

Duffy was number 1 on the field, the boss. Off the field he was ridiculed. Bubba was ignored on the field and was number 1 on the campus, the boss. Everywhere he went, they gathered in swarms, like bees. Mr. Smith gave each bee her due, with Texas respect. One bee never buzzed—her name was Marcia, and she was a WASP. She had two roommates who adored Mr. Smith, and she lived in an apartment above his. "There was a trail of females going in and out, an array of ladies. The music just shook the entire house—every night he had a party," Marcia says. "My roommates, crazy Judy and the other one, gave a party one weekend, and everyone came, including Bubba. In the wee hours of the morning everyone had left, including my roommates, everyone but this awesome black man sitting in the corner. I knew who he was; the entire student body knew who he was." Bubba says, "She was an unusual person. Marcia was tall, slim, and always looked wonderful. She down-played herself, which made her more attractive. I had run across some hard chicks—been through this, been through that—no fault of theirs; but I was tired of this and that, and there was a glow inside of this young lady, a glow I hadn't seen before." They talked quietly that morning, about their lives and hopes. Two young people: one from the North, the other from the Southwest; one wanting nursing, the other football; both had mothers who wanted college for them; both were Christians; and both were tired and saying a respectful good evening at 5 AM, going to their beds and dreaming the same dream.

Two days after the final game of the season, a desperate coach Daugherty called a team meeting. Number 95 didn't want to go—"I didn't think I was in the team's plans"—but his good buddy and roomie, George Webster, talked him into it, and they marched over together, marched over through three feet of the snow that Smith used to love. George, of course, rubbed it in by doing a take-off of Bubba's discovery of how wet it was. His impersonation was very feminine, so very precious. Bubba balled up a ball and blasted big George in his perfect teeth. Picture a six-foot eight-inch giant chasing a creature only three inches shorter down a college campus lane filled with little people laughing at their joy.

When they arrived, they sat at mock attention with other members of the team. The group was faced with a granite-serious coach Duffy Daugherty, who was perhaps trying to recall his coach-of-the-year-award days a decade earlier, trying to forget those nights when his throat hurt from hanging. Bubba began humming "The Very Thought of You," rehearsing a plan he had conceived over a breakfast of chili. "Listen up," shouted the assistant as the coach called off the names, shocking everyone. The list included Webster, Thornhill, Lucas, Summers, Garrett, Richardson, Phillips and Smith, all starting, all members of the first team for the 1965 season.

They reined themselves in for half an hour, how no one could explain. For thirty minutes, through a rah-rah lecture, they contained an explosion, until Daugherty and his staff left. The boats in Lake Michigan, Lake Huron, and Lake Erie dropped anchor when the hooplah began. Eight black Americans on a Big Ten defensive team, the first team. Emancipation at Michigan State had arrived, late as it had in Texas, but better late than never.

Onto the terrace of his apartment he strode, six rocks firmly in hand. It was sunset, and the Michigan sky was a purple-pink wash. The coast was clear. He had checked east, north, west.

He leaned back over the edge of the concrete terrace and began tossing the rocks up onto Marcia's. He waited after each connected with the target. Not a sound from above. The fourth and fifth were lobbed like grenades, and when they hit he mumbled the mock explosion. The sixth, heaved lackadaisically, fell back, hitting him on the forehead. About to react to the blow he heard her voice. *Sheeet* was on his lips, but *who is that?* was in his ear. He quickly forgot his pain. He crooned, "Me." "Me who?" was the reply. "Me, Bubba." "What do you want?" The question was easily answered, with truth, but he thought little of the probable reply; instead he said "I want to sing you a song." "A what?" There was a giggle in her soft voice, but Bubba could not stop now—he was on a roll, and any pause might slow him. "May I sing you a song?" "What song?" He felt goofy, but he was a chip off the old block, and if Smitty could sing "Music, Maestro, Please," he could sing "The Very Thought of You." And he did.

Marcia didn't stop him, as he had planned she would; she made him work. Even when he paused, she refused to utter a sound; and he finished the performance with his arms spread as only an eagle could. The sun had disappeared over the horizon, and they looked into each other, acknowledging communion. That bell began to clang inside of his head, and he began to climb, an effort easier for Bubba than most, yet the terrace hadn't been erected for a three hundred-pound-niggah ascension. Marcia's cool melted when he, having safely reached her apartment, made believe he was falling. She grabbed his arm to save him, and he hooted happily, a happiness shared that evening in conversation. They talked about their families and their lives. "I was brought up in a house surrounded by love. I stepped out of the door and saw only hatred. I didn't understand, and when I don't understand, I just keep moving," he told her.

She made dinner, and before they ate, Bubba said grace. Although they had discussed his budding religious convictions, the simple blessing of their food impressed her. The silence came when Marcia confessed to not enjoying football, or anything connected with the macho world. What could he do? He had always impressed other ladies with his Saturday afternoon exploits. "While you're impressing them, why don't we just enjoy each other's ideas?" The young lady had said it, and from the look in her eyes, she meant it.

Someone wanted to be with him for himself, not for his

exploits on the football field. She's an angel—*but* she's white. A lifetime of warnings echoed in memory, and the news out of the cities had not cooled hatreds. Bubba unfolded himself, stood, and reluctantly said goodnight. Marcia was out of bounds. Nothing but friendship. He wanted to keep just that for now. She was pleased with what they shared that evening; no more was needed or expected. She was his friend.

The spring in this world away from that other reality brought fairy-tale blossoms and hard-nosed football back to the ancient campus of Michigan State University. Bubba had worked hard all winter after learning of his promotion to first team, and his focus was on preparing for the 1965 season. He had organized the magnificent eight—Dayton, Ohio's Drake Garrett; Detroit, Michigan's Harold Lucas; Johnstown, Pennsylvania's Jeffrey Richardson; Orangeburg, South Carolina's James Summers; Anderson, South Carolina's George Webster; and Beaumont's Jess Phillips—into a traveling basketball team. Playing the school's freshman team, the fraternities, and even the prisoners from the Lansing jail, they began to jell as a team. He was using his father's approach to unity, and it seemed to be working.

They all worked hard, so hard that they impressed even themselves! Duffy Daugherty was taking fewer and fewer practice swings with his golf clubs; there were even some who say they saw him take a look in the team's direction. But the defensive unit reported to, and learned from, Henry Bullough, a highly respected coach. Daugherty could, in their thinking, "Play with himself as long as he wants."

Summer break came, though, and the old man, now 20, flew home, new pride growing, to find Nobel Peace Prize-winner, Martin Luther King, Jr., his parents' guest. King, the march from Selma to Montgomery, Alabama, behind him, was touring the country campaigning for the Voting Rights Bill now before the Congress. The Smiths, leaders in Beaumont, were asked for their support and of course gave it. As the Civil Rights leader was leaving, he shook Bubba's hand and wished him well at school. Bubba, like everyone, was impressed by King's simplicity and thanked him for what he had done. Even then Bubba wondered about King's safety. "He was saying things that Negroes couldn't say and stay among the living."

The young Smiths and Beaver's guest, college friend Gayle Sayers, tamed the fear they shared for their leader's life by jumping in a car and going to the beach. The foursome, including Tody, worked out together, Beaver giving valuable advice after each wind sprint. Gayle focused on balance; Bubba and Tody on sheer speed. Gayle ran like a bullet but had a herky-jerky style. Beaver taught Gayle his own dip-and-do method. When Beaver began to run, he decided before he cut, rather than as he cut. An early decision allowed a runner to maintain his speed. Most runners, even the very best, like Gayle, would momentarily stop, do a head fake, then change direction. That moment lost time and allowed the defense to gain a step.

Beaver's method doubled Bubba's speed—his time under fifty yards was as fast as any running back's. Tody had also caught the magic of a great player. Bone-tired, the four would return home every evening whipped but prepared for the future.

September 18 was the beginning of Michigan State's football schedule, and UCLA was in town, sure of victory. Before the game Bubba talked with home boy Mel Farr, and they promised one another they would make All-American together.

The new defensive unit held the team coached by Tom Protho to three points, and someone bet that the UCLA coach would have reconsidered the lackluster invitation he had once made to Mr. Smith after seeing the caliber of the junior's performance—that he would have begged him to come to California then.

A chant began to grow and fill East Lansing that Saturday. The first time he heard it, Bubba hoped it would go on and on. The chant—"Kill, Bubba, kill!" He promised his fans that he would.

Joe Hart of the Saginaw *News* wrote, "A rugged defensive end, Charles Smith, set up the first of Kenney's field goals by recovering a Bruin fumble at UCLA's 19-yard line as Michigan State won, 13–3." The game that followed on September 25 is one that Penn State's coach Roy Engle and halfback Mike Irwin still talk about. Mr. Irwin, a talented junior with Penn State, ran a kickoff fifty-three yards. Bubba, who was behind the racing back, caught him directly in front of the Penn State coach on the sidelines. As he overtook the young man, Bubba was heard to yell, "Where you going?" before he hammered him into the ground. Penn State was shut out by the Michigan State defense. Bob Pille of the Detroit *Free Press* wrote, "When the Lions tried to do anything of their own on offense, they encountered Bubba Smith."

October 2 Michigan State returned to East Lansing, and a growing group of dedicated fans were yelling, "Kill, Bubba, kill!" fifteen minutes before the game began. Michigan State beat Illinois, 22–12. Reporter Bob Frey of the Jackson *Citizen-Patriot* wrote, "The late heroics were made possible by some awesome defensive efforts by such performers as end Bubba Smith and rover back George Webster." He continued, "Smith, who sparkled all afternoon and several times broke into the Illinois backfield to harass quarterback Fred Custardo, blocked a Custardo pass in the final period that Owens intercepted and set up State's final touchdown. . . . Smith also recovered a fumble."

October 9 at Ann Arbor, Michigan. The Michigan State team held their next-door neighbors to a loss of fifty-one yards and won their fourth straight game, 24–7. Wayne DeNeff, sports editor of the Ann Arbor *News* said, "George Webster and Bubba Smith each received the game ball." Quoted coach Duffy Daugherty, "Both Smith and Webster did truly outstanding jobs on the defense for us."

Coach Smith took a day off from his own winning at Charlton Pollard and flew up to see his son play. Woody Hayes, the legendary coach of Ohio State, who had attempted to grab Beaver three years before, warned Smitty that his team would run directly at Bubba October 16, 1965. Joe Hart, the Saginaw *News* reporter, recorded the outcome. "Led by defensive stalwarts Bubba Smith and George Webster, the Spartans accomplished what no team had ever been able to do during Ohio State University's storied gridiron history." They held the Buckeyes to minus twenty-two yards rushing. Add the two games together, and the opposition was held to minus seventy-three yards.

No one reported it, but Smitty laughed in Woody Hayes's face after the game. That evening Bubba called his mama. Georgia was ecstatic but wondered why only twenty-two yards. She also wanted to know how long her husband would leave her alone.

Marcia would not come to any games, yet they were together more and more—many laughs and a few tears. She had told her parents about her new acquaintance, and her mother responded, "Why a black man; you've always had a boy friend?" Marcia questioned her mother. "Do you think white girls only go with blacks when they can't get a white boy friend?" Her mother, who loved her deeply, cried "If you marry him, you'll become black, and I'll never have grandchildren."

Bubba and Marcia sneaked off to a movie, and after the film, Bubba walked five feet behind her. Marcia asked, "What are you doing walking back there?" "You don't want these people to know you're with me, do you?" Bubba replied. "If I didn't want them to know, I wouldn't be here," she shot back. Bub, though, decided to rest the relationship at least until after the season. Marcia hadn't any problem with his plan; all she wanted was him, not a time frame.

At Lafayette, Indiana, Michigan State saved its offense for the final quarter, beating Purdue, 14–10. Before the game the brilliant satirist Ogden Nash had added Bubba Smith to his litany of famous folk.

"When hearing tales of Bubba Smith,
You wonder, is he man or myth?"

Quite a tribute to the Junior from Michigan State, but as you know, all things can be used against you, especially by fans rooting for the other team.

Bubba saw his mama, the visitor this time, sitting there in the sixth row, carefully placed on the 50-yard line by her son's order. They had waved before the game when he heard Doodlebug's whistle screech. It was more than interesting to see the immense quarterback crusher wave to his mama, though. Mad Dog Thornhill was the only member of the team courageous enough to mention Bubba's style in the art of waving. Of course Bubba used his gap to guide a few ounces of saliva toward Mad Dog's face guard after he heard his critique. Purdue fans are Miller Brewing patrons, and the gentleman sitting directly in front of Georgia began misusing Ogden Nash's verse as well as the Miller beer. He shouted that he thought Master Smith was a myth. Mama Smith, like a true Texan was packin' her umbrella, and she decided to test the strength of both the parasol and the fan's head. The blow and the verbal reaction was easily heard on the Michigan State bench, and as the fan turned toward Mama, another fan pointed to the field. Number 95 was climbing over the fence in his direction. The fan decided that he probably had the wrong person and quickly left the stadium to look for the real culprit. Michigan State recorded number six in a row that afternoon.

United Press International had reported that the number-1 team in the nation was President Cecil MacKay's Michigan State team. The next game, "The quarterback rode to my side of the field, jumped to throw; I caught him in midair and knocked him out. I stood over him, and the fans screamed, 'Kill, Bubba, kill!' I raised both hands over my head and screamed louder, 'Yeah!'" They won that seventh game easily, beating Northwestern, 49–7.

On November 6 Bubba returned to a city he had visited in another time. All of the cab drivers recognized him because his face was plastered all over the Iowa newspapers' front pages. In fact six Michigan State team members smiled from those pages, and beneath their pictures read, "Virtually since Michigan State started its seven-game winning streak, such Spartans as George Webster, Clint Jones, Gene Washington, Bob Apisa, Jerry West, and Bubba Smith were cited by the All-American board." "I had a dream, and it came true," Bubba told his proud parents after the game.

A curious moment in college football history took place that game in Iowa. The score was 35–0 in the fourth quarter. Coach Daugherty had replaced his All-Americans, but the Iowa team was driving. Two completed passes put them on Michigan State's nine-yard line.

"Our inspirational leader, Mad Dog Thornhill, raced over to me on the sidelines and announced that we couldn't let Iowa score. Mad Dog said, 'Hey man, Duffy won't let us in. Why don't we all get together and go on the field?'" Bubba quickly rounded up the team and strode onto the field unannounced. Their wide-eyed coach yelled, "Get off!" They were unshakeable and replaced the substitutes. Iowa was first down and ten on the twenty-yard line when the takeover occurred. After the next four plays they found themselves fourth down and fifty-two yards to go. Iowa rushed one yard for the entire game.

It was Indiana's turn at Spartan Stadium. During the game, a tight one, a lineman who was hurting from Bubba's pounding whispered to him, "Don't you fellas play Notre Dame next week?" Bubba shook his helmet yes. The youngster said, "Then listen up. Save it for the Irish. And they did. Notre Dame posted a minus twelve yards at home against the All-Americans from East Lansing. The score: 12–3. Leo Fischer, of Chicago's *American* said, "Michigan State's defense was magnificent. Bubba Smith, George Webster, and Charles Thornhill were so completely in control of the game that on fourteen of the scant forty plays the Irish were permitted to run from scrimmage, the ball carrier wound up with a loss." Ten games, ten wins—a season without a loss.

In preparation for the Rose Bowl Bubba and his teammates soon learned that they would be living, practicing, and getting to know their spirits in a monastery in the California hills. Before he became a monk, however, the professional scouts and coaches had a few discussions with Bubba. They were talking with all the All-Americans, but most of the others had been clear in response to the question, "Are you going to stay in school?" Not an innocent question—those who were not going to stay in college could be drafted by the pros. Mr. Smith purposely fumbled his answer, using Georgia's think-ahead-of-'em technique. His reply to hungry scouts was "I'm not sure. I've got to help my parents, and it costs so much to stay in college." Cold hard cash money in cool white envelopes were now shoved at him—only after he made what he thought was his private joke, did he understand the possibilities of his attitude. He began feeling the same way he had felt when he was the treasurer of his social club in junior high school; but without parents around, who could get hurt? Fifty thousand dollars were offered to him that perfect year.

From presents to piety, he traveled to Duffy's Monastery. "Everyone understood the reasoning, but there were some different kinda dudes on our team. Dudes that didn't need to stay anywhere much less a monastery." Bubba explains. "Some would curse and follow up with 'Oh, forgive me, God!' Some would play cards and say, 'Help me, God!'" Bubba shakes his head in mock frustration. "It got to be a little weird up there, high in the California hills, and some of them were!"

The team practiced, ate, and practiced. "I could tell that Duffy was pissed. Hey man, Steve Juday, our senior quarterback and team cocaptain had broken some Spartan records, with seventy-nine completions out of one hundred forty-eight passes thrown. Gene Washington, Tom Krzemienski, and Dick Gordon helped him break those records, but Duffy wanted his boy in the big time." Bubba could tell by the practice games that the Rose Bowl was to be Duffy's Bowl, and he prayed that he would be right on time with his plan.

The new year came in—1966 was upon us, and the most celebrated squad in sixty-nine seasons of Michigan State competition took the field in Pasadena for the Rose Bowl. The game is annually played between the champion of the Pac-8—in 1966, UCLA—and the winner of the Big Ten. The record for competition between the teams in the Rose Bowl was 2—0, Michigan State, in 1954 and 1956, with coach Daugherty at the helm.

Coach Tom Protho, remembering the loss in the first game of the season, had geared his team for victory. "And were geared for a Steve Juday showcase," moans Bubba. "Daugherty also changed the punt-return man, from Drake Garrett to a little dude named Donald Japinga. Both captains were being massaged."

The first touchdown scored by UCLA, in the second quarter, was made possible by Japinga's fumbling a punt on the Michigan State ten-yard line. Although Steve Juday endured one of the worst games of his brilliant career, Daugherty only pulled him with six minutes remaining in the game. Jimmy Raye entered the game and engineered the scoring. Both State extra points were faked, and both failed. Their first loss, the Rose Bowl game, was due to "politics," says Bubba. "I couldn't understand. My heart was broken. A national championship game lost over somebody's ego. My father played whoever was going to help us win on that given day."

Sid Ziff of the Los Angeles *Times* wrote, "Indubitably, you'd have a better chance to move Mount Wilson than Bubba Smith and George Webster." Harley Tinkeham, *Herald-Examiner* sportswriter said, "The two hundred eighty-eight pound Bubba Smith happens to be the Deacon Jones of the college ranks, boasting enough speed to beat all but a few of the Spartan backs at forty." UCLA's quarterback Gary Beban said, "Nobody hit us harder!"

It was the vacation he needed from football, the university, and Marcia. He bid each farewell; only Marcia cried. He had sent most of his cash gifts home but had kept just enough to purchase some wheels. They were not new wheels, but it was his first Bonneville, and he wanted to show off for the Boomahnt dudes. A successful soon-to-be-twenty-one-year-old All-American man-child left his playland in his latest toy. He floored it and burnt some rubber. Two hundred miles from home, the child fell asleep at the wheel, and the man hit two oak trees.

CHAPTER 6

Angel, Colt, and King

From across the lake, past the black winter trees, came faint sounds of a flute and a voice. While he was still unconscious, he heard the melody. At least he thought he did. He awoke, and it stopped. Silence, but for the Texas birds calling their mates and a sneezing mangy dog, engulfed him. Who was looking over me? he asked himself that misty morning. A few minutes later he climbed out of the wreck. The door on the right side of the car fell off as he slowly eased himself out, his back feeling slightly strained.

He took command of himself, like a lonely sergeant, as soon as his head cleared. Those anatomy classes at school helped him survey his body. Not a scratch. He looked around, hoping to hear what he knew he had heard after the impact. There was only the sneezing dog, who looked at him as if to inquire, Why did you wake me? "Excuse me!" Bubba began laughing, and the dog gathered up his strength and booked. "I walked over to the banged-up trees and picked up my hubcaps. I flagged down a passing mail truck and hitched a ride to the nearest town." He called his father and sold his totaled Bonneville for junk.

Waiting in a gas station in a small town in Texas is an experience. It seemed like two hundred days, those minutes, especially for a six-foot-eight two-hundred-eighty-pound black man. "There might have been a hundred people in this town, and they all found a reason to come to the gas station that morning." He asked politely if they had seen an elderly gentleman named Moses in this neck of the woods. The gent who owned the station, who stood by his rifle every minute that Bubba was there, shook his head slowly from left to right and spat.

Smitty was there faster than you could say dang me. Home they drove, talking and laughing about everything from the Rose Bowl to Marcia. Smitty recoached the game and warned him about his love life. Georgia welcomed him with a bear hug. She had fainted, of course, when she had heard the news, but now her prayers had been answered. Tody, who would join him at Michigan State the next semester, merely smiled at his brother. When he had first heard about the crash, he commented, "The niggah can't drive no way." Now he guided his tongue around the inside of his mouth and said "Hey man, Tody will take a plane!" followed by his full hearty laugh. There was no room for indulgence among the Smith men, as Tody concluded, "Why don't you call up Duffy and have him chauffeur you back?" He left the room, his laughter with him always.

After a steaming pot of mustard greens, black-eyed peas, yams, and a tender steak, Bubba felt like himself again, and the next day he complained that he needed an automobile. Smitty had a friend, and they wheeled over. A brand-new white-on-white Riviera was purchased at a bargain price. The renewed Bubba, more flamboyant since his winning season, thought the Riviera a bit too subtle for a senior, all *everthang*. So Smitty carried him to another of his friends, who gold-leafed each door BUBBA. "It's not gaudy, just right," Charles Aaron stated. "They all know now not to fool with this car 'cause it's Bubba's car!"

Before driving his Bubbacar back to Lansing, he stored away enough sleep to avoid a repeat performance of his mishap, and he found himself alone one morning with his mother. They discussed Marcia. She had heard about the young lady from his phone calls but thought it only a fling. Bubba told her the truth. He loved Marcia but the race thing was more than a problem. After hearing his confession, all Georgia could utter, after a cold chill shot through her body, was "Be careful now, okay? Sweetheart, you're still very, very young." "Yes, ma'am," he answered "I know where they would take it to, Mama. They couldn't just accept it as being love. It'd have to a be a niggah that was infatuated with all white women, but it isn't. I'm not on any gung-ho white chick trip." They exchanged looks—not a word was left to say, just one caring glance.

Before getting back on the road, he dialed Marcia's number, hung up, smoked a Winston, thought it over, and dialed again. It rang three times, and he began to replace the receiver when he heard her answer. They talked about his accident, but Bubba played it down. His new car was mentioned; she was not impressed—Marcia was never impressed by toys or games. What she wanted to tell him concerned them, their friendship. Marcia had gone to her minister, a Methodist, for guidance. She had told him about the match and that her parents, more specifically, her mother, were troubled by her choice. The minister had held her hand and said, "Your parents will come around. They'll accept whomever you love. No one can say what is right or wrong but the Lord. Be absolutely sure it's love." There was a pause, and she asked Bubba if there was anything wrong with what she had done. He replied no weakly, and they bid each other farewell.

On the road again the sleek white machine glided north over the roads of Texas. He concentrated, with a little help from his friends Stevie Wonder and Junior Walker, Stevie blowing "Fingertips" and Walker asking, "What Does It Take (to Win Your Love)?" The only break in his drive came when hunger nudged him off the highway. He began inspecting the restaurants, hoping his senses would steer him straight to a cool one, one that wouldn't ask him to leave because of their race policy. He saw one that didn't appear to be a problem and stopped. One hour later he emerged, wondering how they knew his name. He purchased a newspaper, looked behind him, and tried to figure out his popularity. "The word has spread fast," he thought, closing the gold-leafed doors behind him.

It was 1966 and President Lyndon Johnson began calling America the Great Society. The country's gross national product had risen to six hundred seventy-five billion dollars: it was the headline on the paper. Bubba's mind stayed on money the rest of the drive. Seemingly a controlling force in life, it fascinated him. White people worshipped the stuff. Hadn't they given him fifty thousand dollars as a tip the past year? If fifty grand was a tip, what were his wages?

He guided his Bubbacar past East Crescent Road, past the railroad tracks, along Harrison Road. He made a resounding right on Stadium Road, stuck on Junior Walker and the All-Stars, and "Shotgun" blasted the roof off the car. The index finger of his left hand kept the tempo, pointing with every downbeat. He leaned back, sagging a bit to the right. Bubba had seen his style-king brother Tody do it that way, and it looked hip, so! He floated onto the campus on a white cloud and his black sound. They loved it, his worshippers were thrilled. On a bannister sat brother Tody, who had flown in, both of his thumbs in the air, greeting his HNIC (head niggah in charge) and BMOC (big man on campus) brother Bub.

Tody's focus was a bit different than the dozen or more coeds who surrounded their returning hero. His eyes were focused on the coeds, as well as the car. He knew Bubba; he had not been formally introduced to the Riviera or the ladies. "Hey man, thanks," Tody said, wearing a tilted, stingy-brim hat, a cashmere sports jacket, scarf, and slacks. Bubba opened his trunk and began removing his suitcases. "Help me, Tode," implored Bubba. "All these lovely ladies, and you ask your baby brother for assistance. Damn Charles." Tody was using his white voice, which started in his throat and sounded very proper.

Bubba was trying not to laugh. His first day on campus and already El Toro was talking shit. "Just let Tody assist them keys from those huge paws, big brother man. There are some females on this campus who would give up anything to ride in style with their hero's baby brother, anythang!" "No," moaned Bubba, "I should have told you what Beaver told me in Iowa." "Too late—they love their little Tody, doncha darlin'." Little Tody, standing six feet six inches and weighing two hundred fifty pounds, firmly held two giggling sisters, and they were in seventh heaven.

Bubba was delighted to have his brother with him. El Toro forced everyone to relax. There was pride also—Bubba thought highly of his brother's talent. He often said in interviews that Tody would soon be better than he was. No one believed him, but Bubba was as serious about his brother's talent as he was about his own.

He was about to show Tody the hot spots on campus, but Tody and the coeds drove away in Bubba's car.

After he had settled in, then, he went to Marcia's apartment. A winter sky, more ominous than usual, hurried his final steps to her door. The door opened as their hearts had; the enchantment of the afternoon, however, quickly vanished when Bubba flatly refused to meet her parents. "If they said something wrong, what would I do?" She couldn't answer, and all

Georgia Oreatha Curl

 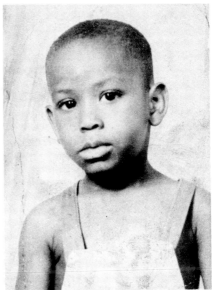

Left, Willie Ray "Doll" Smith; right, Charles Aaron "Bubba" Smith

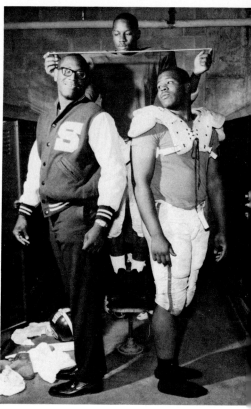

Left, The Smith Stance—Willie Ray "Beaver" Smith, Jr., at Iowa; right, senior Bubba Smith and freshman Lawrence Edward "Tody" Smith at Michigan State

Michigan State coach Duffy Daugherty

Michigan State All-Americans (left to right): Bob Apisa, Clinton Jones, Bubba, Gene Washington, and George Webster

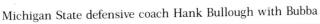

Michigan State defensive coach Hank Bullough with Bubba

Notre Dame's Terry Hanratty seconds before his shoulder is dislocated by number 95, Bubba Smith, in "The Game of the Century."

Left, The Rams' Roman Gabriel tries the impossible against Bubba as number 75, Deacon Jones, takes notes; right, Bubba at Baltimore

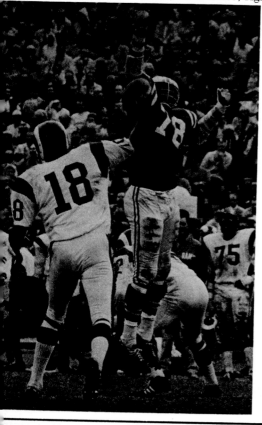

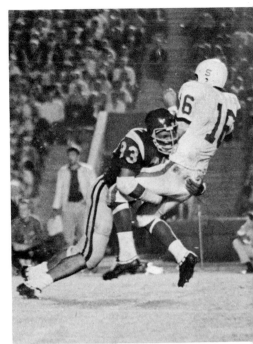

USC's Tody Smith sacks Stanford's Jim Plunkett

The Smiths of Houston—a warm family; Tody Smith, number 85, at Houston

Left, A crippled Bubba talks it over with Roger Staubach; right, Tody Smith at Houston

At Houston, Bubba talks to his first coach, his father

Number 77, Bubba Smith, in action against the Cincinnati Bengals

Left, Tody Smith with dam Khiana; right, Stanley "the Counselor" Cohen

Bubba in Beaumont with Mama

she felt was an emptiness. He left her—it was now dark—and the Blizzard of the Century began that very evening. Cold, arctic air had mixed with warm, moist air from the Gulf of Mexico, causing gale-force winds and heavy snow. Mixing is a monster when it's against the rules.

The spring brought telephone calls from panting scouts and coaches, who drooled to sign the all-everythang Smith. The most interesting call came from an important scout for an American Football League team all hush-hush and low tones. The drama of it interested the bored twenty-one-year-old, who flew to the rendezvous. If nothing else, he could always use a free trip and hang with his Beaumont partners, Harvey "Chili Red" Dixon, Brill Cream, and Poochie White.

It was Chili Red who drove him to the raggedy, old hotel in north Tennessee. The joint looked as if Humphrey Bogart and Sounder were lurking around the corner. He walked through the rusted wrought-iron doors and went straight to room 117, knocked, and was let in by the scout himself. After the greeting, they sat down and began talking deal, a million-dollar contract to sign with his team in 1967. Smith poked at his glasses and read every word. When he finished, he calmly shook his head no. "I had learned something from the Sammies—never take the first offer!" he later said. Undaunted, though slightly stunned, the scout removed a second document from his natty briefcase. "If you don't want to sign the contract, sign this release form!" It stipulated that if Smith chose the American Football League, he could play only for the scout's team. Accompanying the document was an envelope, which contained ten thousand dollars. Bubba counted, signed, accepted, shook hands, booked, and partied till dawn with his partners.

There was that look in his eyes, and he was hot. "If you don't give back the money you're off the team" the official said.

"What money?" asked Bubba, looking as much like an angel as number 95 could.

"Even when you give back the money, I want an apology to the full team."

"A wot?"

"You heard me!"

"Hey man, I don't have any money or apologies to give

to anyone. If you put me off the team, I'll go to Canada, wait for my class to graduate, and then go into the pros!"

Bubba stood and began to walk. If the official could have seen the twinkle in his eye, and if he had a better wristwatch, he would have let him walk through the door and waited; but he didn't see, and he seemed not to be able to tell time. He stopped Bubba and drew back his threat, at least half of it. He could stay on the squad but he would have to apologize. Bubba, the prince of hurrah, knew who had all the aces, and he rubbed it in, just a hair.

"Oh, you must have heard of a Dodge Dart. Three of my partners have."

"Giving anyone anything on the Michigan State campus is against NCAA rules!"

"You're telling me that I have to apologize to the team 'cause I don't have a Dodge Dart? Is that it?" Bubba looked down at the red-faced official and waited for his reply.

"Let's forget the matter, Smith, and remember, do not accept money while you're at this university!"

"Yes, sir" Bubba said, straight-faced. He went out, traded in his Bubbacar and bought an Eldorado. After he drove the gleaming Cadillac to his dormitory, he spread the word that he had gotten it free. His Dart-gifted friends were crazy with jealousy.

Coach Duffy Daugherty canceled spring training for his All-Americans, Webster, Washington, Apisa, West, and Smith. The coach needed time to inspect his sophomores and juniors. So, after private workouts, Bubba would pedal his Eldorado around the campus, tapes blasting away, enjoying the world before he had to kill-Bubba-kill, and dreaming about his future. Once he interrupted practice, his Eldorado screeching to an angled stop. Number 95 jogged over to Jimmy Raye, the team's new starting quarterback. He poked Jimmy in his chest, pretending to get on his friend's case, and said, "Don't worry now, little dark dude—when you become a senior, an All-American and All-Big Ten, you won't have to work so hard to make the team." Raye, a junior, fell on his knees laughing, and Bubba boogied off the field and bopped his Eldorado away. Mr. Raye relaxed, as did the rest of the squad, remembering that number 95 was still around.

On June 8, 1966, the American and National football leagues agreed to end their competition for talent and merge. Great news for the leagues; the worst news for any college player. Joe Namath, once quarterback for the University of Alabama, had reportedly received four hundred thousand dollars from the Jets in 1965. Donny Anderson, Texas Tech running back, had signed a record seven-hundred-thousand-dollar contract with the Green Bay Packers. Now it would be back to GO, with hard negotiating.

Their shared heartbreak united George Webster and Bubba. Bubba, who had been sure his million-dollar contract would be topped, had nonchalantly pushed all of that cash away, and he was sick. George also knew the golden door had been but six months away. There was no time for anything but preparation for the season, a season that had to be their ultimate effort, now the golden door had been partially shut. The teams could not drop salaries that drastically: if both of them finished among the top first-round draft picks, most of their money would be salvaged. It was all or nothing in the fall of 1966. Other incentives included pride and the big ol' diamond ring received for winning the national championship. They parted with a firm handshake, two All-Americans ready to take on the rock.

A rock might have been easier to swallow than the letter that had been neatly placed in one of his shirt pockets. His mind was spinning like a top with career problems, mistakes, and probabilities. He unfolded the letter, shook his brain loose, took a deep sigh, and slowly read—Marcia had had it. If she was serious, he thought, it shouldn't end with a note. What will be, will be, but in person. He was at her door in a few minutes (the knock even felt final to his knuckles). No answer, and he leaned close to the door and heard the sobbing. She had been betrayed by the ignorance of her country, the fear of her parents, and the divided love of the man she loved. "Open the door, Marcia," he asked. There was a lonely silence, and he repeated his request with a bit more bass in his voice. A sob cracked the distance between them, once only skin, now a locked door. "If you don't open it, I'll break it." No huff or puff in his voice, only pure love. A moment later it opened. "We'll work it out!" he lied.

"You can't handle it!" she whispered.

"Just like that?" His voice was lighter now. "You can't do that."

"I just did," she said, and she had. Bubba knew in his mind it was for the best; his heart disagreed. His common sense held fast, though, and he backed off and left his heart with her.

There were no notes for Lawrence Edward, just letters. One was an A, the other an F. The A was bestowed in his golf class. After his instructor saw Frank "Sweet" Foreman, Don "Snap" Law, and Tody hit their golf balls perilously near the grand windows of the university, the negotiating talent of the middle-aged man, who had already complained of ulcers, came into play. "I'll give you and your friends an A if you never return to class." Tody was pleased.

The F pissed him off. A failure in humanities. Lawrence could not believe it. After spending his cherished time writing a conclusive study that challenged society's usage of race and color in reference to good and evil, they failed him. "The paper was excellent," he said. The stern but feminine professor said flatly, "You didn't write it." Tody has a tendency to hide his brilliance with brashness: he had shown this lady professor one side of himself, and she had accepted it as the complete package. What angered him was that he had done his time and had had fun writing the paper, a rare occasion indeed, but true, all true, truly.

To add insult to injury, defensive coach Hank Bullough, highly respected by Bubba, said to Tody, about his professor, "That type woman is the kind that you want for your mother." A man must take care in using the word *mother* before a huge, volatile, athletic black man, especially one who needs to erase an F from his soul. El Toro saw red, and when Bullough heard the lock on the classroom door click shut, he realized how matadors must feel. The ferocious one slid a desk toward the locked door, carefully removed his cashmere jacket, and gently placed his professional pool cue on a chair. Before any blows could be struck, another assistant coach, Gordon Seer, intervened. Seer had muscled open the door, discussed the future, made a few jokes, and attempted to calm the rage in less than three minutes. Tody respected Seer, and a long last moment saw peace return.

Duffy Daugherty talked with freshman Smith after the incident, and during the lecture on conduct, he was reported to say that he understood "nigras" and hoped that Lawrence Edward would adapt to the Spartan tradition. It was the first time in his eighteen-year life that Tody had heard the word *nigra*.

Tody knew what it denoted but could not believe that he had traveled from Texas poverty to Michigan splendor to hear it. He waited a moment to hear a punch line; none came. Freshman Smith put on his jacket, picked up his pool cue, excused himself, and went out and won two hundred dollars from the Michigan State students with his cue stick.

I want to be part of the group, the most-talked-about collegiate football player in the country thought. He was frightened, because he had paid the price of emotional pain in high school. A friend, Rudy Lucas, brought him to the Omega frat, where all the ballplayers had pledged, and he was interviewed. "Could a Big Brother call you at 7:00 AM to have his apartment cleaned?" A head shaking no answered. "What would you do if he did?" "Break his neck," he replied simply. "If you had two girls, and a Big Brother wanted one, would you share?" Before Bubba walked out, he asked, "Can't the Big Brother get his own?"

Another invitation was issued to Smith by Gary Kleinman, to pledge his fraternity, Sigma Alpha Mu, better known as Sammie. There Bubba met nice people who had good manners and seemed as vulnerable as he was beneath his BMOC front. The Sammies were competing with another fraternity, the ZBT's, known on campus as Zillion, Billion, and Trillion. The name of course interested Smith, always thinking of the future, but he had felt the Sammies' warmth and had made up his mind. The group wanted him—it was a feather in their collective cap to have the talented football player. No other six-foot eight-inch guys were in the group, and a genuine friendship was growing. The house mother, "Mom" Lewis, became his Georgia away from home. They talked for hours. "She was always honest—I loved her," says Bubba. He manned the phones when they called him, but practice kept him so busy that he had to become an honorary member. He always found time for Mom Lewis, though.

The 1966 football season began, despite coach Daugherty's vocabulary, and his team, rated number 1 in the nation, was ready. Ready also was the number-1 end in college football, loose, large, and lovable. He found out the visiting team's schedule and drove his Eldorado over to where their bus emptied and parked. His carefully chosen parking space was directly across from the bus door. The door opened, and senior Smith raised the sound level of his radio. "P-u-l-e-a-s-e, Pulease," shouted James Brown. "Baybee, pulease don't go!"

Each player flipped his head toward the colossal All-American leaning against his expensive car, a frozen smile on his face. They took double and triple takes and hastened toward the locker room. They disappeared, but the music played on.

That Saturday, September 17, Joe Hart of the Saginaw *News*, after witnessing the season's first game, wrote "Spearheaded by George Webster and Charley Bubba Smith, two sure-fire repeat All-Americans in this era of defensive platoons, Michigan State handcuffed the North Carolina defense." The score was 28–10. September 25, Detroit *Free Press*, Jack Berry: "They lost their quarterback Jack White on the second play when big Bubba Smith blasted by a blocker and slammed White to the ground for a four-yard loss. . . . Big Bubba, who stands about as tall as Beaumont Tower [a building on Michigan State's campus], played one of his finest games. The senior threw Penn State backs for losses four times."

The excitement that only Duffy and Bubba could create happened later in the year. Michigan State had won five straight, and they were getting ready to win the Big Ten crown by knocking over Purdue. The press had a field day. "The coach was performing like a lion tamer," says Bubba. "We were warming up, A squad against B, and when we rushed, I stopped before I reached the backup quarterback and barely touched him. Duffy began hooping it up for the news dudes and openly reprimanded me. 'Is that the way you're going to hit Griese?' he yelled. I just looked at him. Why would I hit anyone, especially Larry Lukasik, who was a member of our team?" questioned number 95. "If I had gone in and hit Larry, they would have questioned my sanity and removed my ass from practice. But Duffy kept it up for fifteen solid minutes, and I was fuming hot. I fired up and hit the guy. Lukasik, who was wondering what my problem was, threw the ball at my head as I returned to the huddle. Before I could stomp Lukasik, I felt this tug on my jersey from behind. I hoped it was who I thought it was, and I let go a backhand left. I was right, and Duffy reeled back, looking very much like a blowfish," smiles Smith. "He screamed at me to get off the field. The walk from the practice field to the locker room behind Spartan Stadium is over two hundred yards. I tried to mark each step with an article of clothing. First went the helmet of course, then the jersey, the pads, the T-shirt, the pants. The flashbulbs were popping. I was finally down to my jock when I disappeared into the locker room. My first stripper gig," cracks Bubba. "If Duffy wanted ink, he should have tried that."

Smith didn't attend practice the next day; he was busy with the Temptations when Danny Boisture, the assistant coach knocked, opened, and respectfully requested his presence on the field. "I waited till the end of side 1 and happily left with him."

A writer who probably had seen Ogden Nash's verse, Tom Fitzpatrick of the Chicago *Daily News,* needed a story, and the headline read, BUBBA SMITH, 285 POUNDS OF MYTH. At dinner that evening Duffy read the newspaper story to forty players. Duffy was plainly irritated at the writer—He used words like *totally inaccurate, almost libelous.* When he finished, said an East Lansing newspaperman, Harry Stapler, he turned to Bubba and offered him the newspaper. "I don't want it," clipped Bubba. "I want his behind."

During the next game easily won by State, 22–0, Bubba made a tackle and leaned over to the running back, Larry Gates, and said, "Let me introduce you to the myth." The fans screamed, "Kill, Bubba, kill!"—in an away game.

Nine games, nine victories, and the team was back home at Michigan State. The only close score was against Ohio State, a game played in a driving rainstorm. MSU had won by three points; because of that score Notre Dame, a winner of nine games, placed first in the National ratings by the wire services.

Second was not a word to be found in the Michigan State vocabulary. The team and the awesome student body were fighting mad, and the superpowers were scheduled to play Saturday. Emotion on the Michigan State campus was ignited on Monday—the media began to transform a sporting event into a race issue. Some described the game as Notre Dame versus Grambling. Grambling is a black university and the sick comparison referred of course to the number of black Americans on the Michigan State team.

Intense practice began in the crisp chill at 2:30 PM that Monday. The team closed its ranks, proudly demonstrating a new-found pride in the finest university in America. It was their final game of the season. For the seniors, including number 95, it was their last hurrah as collegians. Over the rainbow was a pot of gold in professional football. Everything that they had worked for was six days away. Everyone knew it and showed it on the first day of practice. They worked for themselves and each other. During the session Bubba advised Jim Summers, "Hey man, if the sweep [the offensive movement] starts my way, I'll take out everythang and everybody; you make the tackle." After seeing Bubba's performance at practice, Summer asked, "Bub, why don't you slow the runner down too?"

Everywhere that week emotion was building. "Kill 'em Bub!" "Kick ass big fella!" "Do it for us!" Notre Dame effigies were burning everywhere. The grill, the streets, classrooms, corridors, dormitories—the city was on fire with passion. Classes were cancelled; pep rallies were everywhere on campus and held morning, noon, and night.

After practice it was films, films and more films. The image of the Notre Dame team swirled through the mind of every Michigan State player—Notre Dame's tendencies, Notre Dame's patterns, Notre Dame's switches. The conversation at every meal was Notre Dame, Notre Dame, Notre Dame. Never a letup, no escape, one objective: to win.

On Wednesday, after a brutal practice, Bubba went to his room on the ground floor of Wonders Hall. He needed to relax, away from the team and students. As he closed his eyes, he began to hear a faint chanting. "Kill, Bubba, kill!" At first he thought it must be his mind playing tricks on him—this, the third day of the buildup, and everything he had done was involved with football. It came again—"Kill, Bubba, kill!"—louder this time, again and again. John Gorman, his roommate, went to the window, opened it, and his mouth dropped open. Bubba raised himself from his bed and walked to the window. Six thousand students, every race, creed, and color, had joined hands and were chanting "Kill, Bubba, kill!" He waved, and the screams rose. Someone hollered, "Speech, speech."

"What could I say?" he remembers. "I cleared my throat and began. 'Er . . . ahm . . .'" Before he could continue, six thousand young people roared their approval. As swiftly as they came, they left—all they wanted was to see him. "Damn, they could have listened to my little talk," he said laughingly to Gorman, but that time, those moments, changed Bubba. "Those beautiful people were depending on me. The university that had opened my eyes to life was watching me. I would show my gratitude Saturday." The game had become bigger than life.

Searching for relaxation, he went to visit a young lady. Twenty minutes of foreplay and about to shift into high gear and her lovely face was transformed into that of the not-so-lovely Terry Hanratty, the Notre Dame quarterback. "I was beginning to trip. Damn, do you believe the timing? I had to go."

Thursday CBS followed Bubba and Jimmy Raye, then the MSU quarterback and now the assistant coach of the Los Angeles Rams, around the campus. A camera whirled and recorded every move—leaving the practice field, walking and talking on campus, signing autographs. "They even had me open a textbook in my room. When I opened the book, the page transformed itself into a football field." There was no relief. "I had been treated like a demigod for two years, and I couldn't let them down now!"

Thursday practice was defense day, picking up keys day—a key is a clue to what is about to happen—and they were trained to notice every movement and tendency and variation before it happened. Concentration razor-sharp, every sense tripled, Bubba was no longer cool and laid-back; he was a land mine ready to explode at the faintest touch.

"Friday came, and I decided to do my usual intimidation of the visiting squad. I asked Jimmy Raye to join me. It was Eldorado time. The week had us crazy with competition, and if the Notre Dame offensive line saw me, all three hundred twenty pounds, well, there might be a hard night's sleep in store for them. It had worked before; why not this game?"

Off they went, tingling with intensity, burning rubber on Grand River Drive. Another automobile joined them on that short drive. The car wasn't as stylish as Bubba's, but it had a few frills that Bubba's didn't, including lights on the roof, and the lights were twirling. "I thought they were wishing us well for the game," he says. The gentlemen in blue, however, had other plans. Bubba was pulled over, notified he had fifteen hundred dollars in traffic tickets outstanding, and a warrant had been issued for his arrest. He was handcuffed. "Do you realize that we have a game tomorrow?" The cop deadpanned with a chill, "Michigan State has a game tomorrow; you're coming to jail!" Jimmy Raye, thoroughly confused, was asked by Bubba to tell Duffy.

In jail he became the focus of attention of the inmates. "What's happening, Bub?" "Hey Dude, gonna see ya on the tube tomorrah!" "My main man, what is shaking?" What was shaking was Smith's head, and not in the way he was asked. Bars and three blank walls surrounded him, and they were closing in fast. "Two hours later I heard yelling down the hall, in the front of the jailhouse. I recognized the voice of Biggie Munn."

Mr. Munn, the athletic director of MSU, was in excellent voice. "Do you like your job," he asked the police chief. Minutes later a nonchalant Bubba was released.

About to be secluded in the Kellog Center Hotel on campus for the evening, a frustrated lover attempted to ease himself with a few strokes of good luck with a young lady, who, a feverish fan of her school team, told Bub, "Save your energy for tomorrow!" A strange week indeed.

At the hotel, the offense in one room, the defense in another, the coaches were as spirited as the team. More films were shown, and in the middle of one, the projector was stopped, and the lights flicked on. Hank Bullough pointed to Jess Phillips, the team's starting safety. "Terry Hanratty rolls out, runs to the sideline, stops, comes back to midfield, which allows the receiver to run a post pattern [down and in]. When Seymour is in the open, he turns to look for the ball. When he turns, I want you to take his head off. We'll accept the fifteen-yard penalty, but Seymour will be looking for you every time they run it. That play is the play they won nine games with. If they beat us, they won't with this play." The mumbling of the other defensive men began—they wanted a green light also. "Tell me once, just once," begged Thornhill. Bullough ran the film again and again, stopping it only to allow Jess to digest the timing.

Bubba began the rhythmic claps.

Two claps: "Jess, you got to hurt him, baby."

Two claps: "Do it, Jess."

Two claps: "Don't let the white boy run over you."

Two claps: "Jess, you got to knock his mother-fuckin' head off."

Two claps: "You can get it, Jess."

On and on it went, until not only Jess but the entire room was on fire. "Right there, Jess," Bullough repeated as the film showed Seymour cutting toward midfield in front of an opposing safety. It was the safety's assignment. Jess was the safety. Jess was now a true madman. A killer.

After the formations were repeated, they were dismissed and asked to return to their rooms, to sleep the sleep of champions.

ND Day was upon them. By 7:00 AM most had showered, dressed, and were ready. The defensive team had their own meeting. The last time they had played Notre Dame was a year ago, and they had held them to a total of twelve yards gained, minus twelve yards on the ground, twenty-four in the air. The pass play to Seymour was the problem. Phillips knew his assignment but had to know when the play would occur; he had to be told seconds before. Summers was chosen the Paul Revere, the call man. When Jim saw the formation take shape, he would alert Jess, and then it was search and destroy. They joined hands and went to breakfast.

The game began in 25 degree weather, perfect for football. Nerves relaxed after the first licks. When the Notre Dame formation changed, Sum yelled at Jess as the ball was snapped. **Hanratty**'s favorite target, Jim Seymour, made his cut in, running at top speed. Jess aimed and threw a forearm at his face. Seymour fell like he'd been shot—it was smelling salts time.

Near the end of the first half—MSU ten up—Hanratty ran a play toward Smith. George Webster broke through the line. Hanratty spun away. Mad Dog grabbed him but Terry kept his balance. Then Bubba left his feet, diving with all his force, enough to dislocate **Hanratty**'s shoulder. The star quarterback was finished for the day.

His replacement was Coley O'Brien. Who? A frown appeared on Hank Bullough's brow. The game plan had been set for Hanratty. The MSU defense attempted to make the adjustment, but by the time they caught on, Notre Dame had scored a field goal, and Coley O'Brien had passed for a TD. The score was tied, 10–10.

The final minutes of the game shocked the Michigan State team. Legendary coach Ara Parseghian had lost his will to win and had decided to settle for a tie. He ordered his team to sit on the ball, to use the clock up by spending too much time in the huddle. Rather than play the game, his quarterback ran and fell on the ball. "I couldn't understand why a great coach from a great university wouldn't try to win!" says Bubba. The Michigan State players were screaming at the Notre Dame team. Bubba's "You faggots don't want to win?" was joined by Mad Dog's "Does your mother know you're a punk?"

These All-Americans, five on Michigan State's first team, six on Notre Dame's, were stymied by a coach's decision to be content with a tie. The gun sounded, the game that Duffy Daugherty described as "the best game of the decade" ended without a winner. ABC-TV called it the Game of the Decade, and the Chicago *American* billed it the Game of the Century.

The finest week in Bubba Smith's playing career had ended

in a draw. Bubba and his teammates fell into depression. Two brilliant years—winning nineteen, losing one—and now the final game was a frustrating tie. The next week Notre Dame rolled over USC, 56–0, and were named national champs by both AP and UPI, but number 95 felt that Parseghian was a hope-to-die chump, who didn't deserve the title. National champions should be men.

The Big Ten does not allow its champion to compete in the Rose Bowl in two consecutive years. Number 95's collegiate career was over, and the pleading scouts gave it up: sixty thousand dollars in cash was handed over to the man who had come of age. "Kill, Bubba, kill!" Bubba Smith was awarded All-Big Ten and consensus All-American for the second year, named Lineman of the Year, and to the North-South all-star game. Even in that context he was the most valuable player.

KILL, BUBBA, KILL! read the posters and signs that obscured the buildings of the campus of Michigan State, March 1967, and everyone at the university wished their favorite good luck in the pro draft. This was expected, yet the unexpected occurred as well: the Baltimore Colts had obtained the first draft pick from New Orleans in a trade that had sent quarterback Gary Cuozzo and offensive lineman Butch Allison to the Saints in exchange for linebacker Bell Curry and the first and third draft choices; and because coach Don Shula had been impressed by Bubba's job in the North-South game, the Colts had used the first draft pick to select him, over all the collegiate players. Bubba had been chosen before the Heisman Trophy–winner Steve Spurrier and Purdue's quarterback Bob Griese. Not even Duffy Daugherty had expected that.

"All you heard was Spurrier, Spurrier, Spurrier. Then some of the football people started talking to Bubba. They all found out about Bubba's intelligence, his knowledge of the game, and his desire to play. They realized what a sensitive and serious person he was," declares Bubba's lawyer, Marty Blackman.

(Bubba had met Marty in New York during a weekend when he had appeared with all the other All-Americans, including home boy Mel Farr, on the *Ed Sullivan Show*. Although a friend of his from Michigan State had warned Bubba to watch out for fast-talking Jews in New York, he liked Blackman. Bubba told him what his friend had said, and they joked about Marty's last name as well as about Bubba's Jewish fraternity. Marty Blackman laughed hysterically and became his good friend and agent.)

When the announcement came, the phone rang off the hook. The first call came from his favorite coach at Michigan State. "Henry Bullough, the defensive line coach of the Spartans, a man who Bubba learned to hate and love in those golden years. It was Bullough the Bull who pushed Bub to the limit and then heaved him some more, until the product was gold," wrote Joe Falls. "I'm coming out of retirement because I know all your weaknesses and I'll push you around," Bullough said to Bub.

They all deserved gold, and that was exactly what they wanted. Smith was first, and George Webster second, headed to the Houston Oilers. Gene Washington was third, Clinton Jones fourth, both drafted by the Minnesota Vikings. I'm going to miss these guys, especially Clint, George, Gene, and Mad Dog. Four years is a lot of time. Been thinking about playing against Clint and Gene—don't like it, Bubba thought. After everyone celebrated, he was alone again. The brothers, friends, players, reporters, and agents had left, and he walked over to the phone and dialed the number of his people, who had made him keep his promise to himself. Georgia and Smitty talked to him for hours. When he finished, he dialed Moses' number, and he was out, probably moving someone.

When Martin Blackman, Esquire, in charge of contract negotiations, began trusting Bubba's financial instincts, they set some theatrics in motion. Smith sat in on the clickering, bickering, and slickering. Whenever he heard something he agreed with, he would thump the papers he held in his hands. The sign gave Marty the right to agree to the figure, if he thought it would work legally. The "tennis match" was a pain in the ass for Smith. His idea of himself was not as a product, but he was still learning how *they* did things. One moment in the proceedings joyfully destroyed the solemnity of the meetings: Bubba heard an offer he loved, he thumped, leaned back proudly, and fell off his chair. Their laughter surprised him— he thought that except for Marty they all were robots.

From the negotiations, he reported to the college all-star camp in Chicago, to prepare for the game against the Super Bowl champions. His contract with the Colts had included employment by Baltimore of Willie Ray, Jr., and Willie Ray, Sr. Bubba's father was scouting, and Beaver was to play in the Colts' backfield. Bubba called the Colt training camp every night to hear the news about Beaver. His contact at the camp, an idol of his, Lenny Moore, who Bubba had met when he had attended the Colt rookie camp, reported that Beaver was the best he had ever seen in the game. Bubba relaxed and began concentrating on the all-star game.

Cameron Snyder, a Baltimore newspaperman, came over to Bubba in the dressing room a week before the game and asked him, "Did you hear that Beaver's been cut?" Bubba had just talked with Lenny the night before, and everything had sounded fine. Now Bubba was hot and told the newsman that he didn't want to play anymore. "You'll miss so much," Snyder said.

"Can't miss what you haven't had! I'm happy—what else is there?"

The headline in the paper the next day reported in bold, black letters, BUBBA NOT PLAYING ALL-STAR GAME. When the National Football League read the story the phone lines got as hot as America's black ghettos were that summer of 1967. The black troubleshooter of the league was ordered to talk Bubba into playing. His knock on the hotel door was gentle but firm. The unlocked door opened, and there stood a short man Bubba recognized as the legendary running back of the old football New York Yankees, Buddy Young. Smith smiled through memories of the man's great years. He had been among the first black football players in the professional game. Young lit a cigarette and wiped his sweaty brow. "Mr. Young, what can I do for you?" said Smith.

"Just wanted to give you a helping hand, Bubba," said Young, a cigarette butt dangling from his lower lip. Young continued, "If you play in the game, there are ways of getting Willie Ray reinstated to the Baltimore squad." He went on and on and promised every shortcut if Bubba won most valuable player of the all-star match. Bubba enjoyed the fact that a retired black football player could have as much pull as Buddy Young professed to have, and he believed him. They shook hands, the second cigarette butt stuck to Young's lip.

Bubba ushered Young out, and the phone rang—it was Smitty. Bubba, happy to hear his father's voice, settled back on his bed, expecting to have a long chat with his Beaumont partner, but Smitty startled Bubba by saying, "I'm downstairs." Minutes later Smitty smiled in and shook hands with his beleaguered son. "What you planning on doing, Bubba?"

"First, tell me how you got here?"

Smitty sat down in one of those odd-looking chairs in all

hotel suites, straightened his leg, and started talking. Sounding very much like the Coach Smith of yesteryear, he said, "Now look, the Colts messed over Beaver, we all know that. Maybe something can be done, maybe not—"

Bubba cut in. "How did you get here? Why didn't you tell me you were coming?" Before he could blurt out a third question, Smitty replied, "They called me this morning. The ticket was waiting for me at the airport."

"Who?" yelled Bubba.

"The National Football League! They asked me if I could do anything to get you to play on Sunday."

"Smitty, Buddy Young just left. He told me that if I made MVP for the game, Beaver would play for the Colts this year."

"What are you going to do?"

"I have no idea."

"Let me help, Bubba. Have you thought about Tody? If you play and do well, it will establish Tody when his time comes. He's having problems with his ankle now, but I'm going over to the school from here and straighten all that out."

"I want to help everyone, Smitty, but how will playing this game help anything?" Bubba was standing now near the window of the suite, staring out at 97-degree heat of Chicago and the sailboats on Lake Michigan. Beyond that body of water was his home the past four years, and if he thought it was confusing there . . . the games people play. The image of Buddy Young's cigarette dangling from his lower lip returned, floating on the window pane. Smitty and Bubba were smoking now. Bubba turned and said, "Let's trust Young." His head bobbed up and down in agreement with himself. "I'll do it for Tody."

When he jogged onto the field that warm Sunday evening, stars adorned his jersey and the fans greeted him more than warmly. The awesome Green Bay Packers were the enemy, and the pack had won the Super Bowl for the second season in a row. Bart Starr was on top of his game, and the signs in the stands read BUBBA KILL THE STARR!

The very first play numbers 75 and 64 played Mexican standoff with number 95. Forrest Gregg, six feet four inches, two hundred fifty pounds, and Jerry Kramer, six feet three inches, two hundred forty-five—when they hit, smoke billowed up. Gregg said to Bubba, "Welcome, rook." Bubba replied, "You gonna have to welcome me every play."

The objective was achieved. Smith had a great game, even reaching Mr. Starr once. The most valuable player was number

95, and he waved to his father as the cheers met him—"Kill, Bubba, kill!"—perhaps for the last time. Green Bay had clobbered his team, but this was for Tody and, he hoped, Beaver.

Rick Volk and Bub winged their way to Baltimore the next morning. The training camp was in Westminster, Maryland, and they arrived on time at the uniform fitting. Receiving your togs is no big thing, but Bubba was surprised that his name was printed on a tape pasted to his helmet—the rook junk was getting a little out of hand. Everyone knew Bubba Smith, and he ripped off the tape.

His interest lagged in head gear; more important was the thoughts that were in his head. When he saw Beaver, he learned the answer to his basic question. In a few minutes he discovered his trust in Buddy Young had been misplaced. Young had fulfilled not one of his promises. Was Young an Uncle Tom for the NFL? Coach Don Shula tapped him on the back then and asked, "Why aren't you dressed for the scrimmage game?" Bubba looked at him—had the man forgotten what Bubba had done just sixteen hours ago. "I played a game last night," he replied and walked away.

The next day Shula called an Oklahoma Drill, one man against another. The object was to take the other man out of his path. Number 71, Dan Sullivan, six feet three inches and two hundred fifty pounds, yelled, "I want the big fella." The new number 78—no longer was Bubba number 95—never smiled, merely recognized the challenge. The very first play, and he was in Sullivan's chest. He floored him, for Beaver, floored him good.

Only Lenny Moore and Jim Parker had spoken to him—two greats with nothing else to prove, willing to share their friendship and their greatness. Everyone else on the team was drawn up into unseen ranks. The Baltimore Colts were among the best in professional football. "When you're the best, you share it," Bubba had learned from his father. Bubba had also discovered over the years that screaming and yelling at anyone or anything, even children, never got the job done. From noise only fear may grow. Don Shula was a screamer, and the Colts were afraid to share their greatness.

Ritual was part of the training camp. At lunch the first week someone called, "Bonus baby on the table. Bubba get up and sing your school song!" Maybe it's a way of breaking the wall of silence, he thought. "On the banks of the old Red Cedar," he began, singing the Michigan State song. Only Lenny gave him a nudge and a smile; no ice thawed. At dinner it happened again. "Let's hear it, Smith." This time Bubba shook his head no. "You got my first and last song at lunch time." he said. "Get up," demanded a Colt. The bonus baby glanced around the room with his horn-rimmed eyes and said, "Unless somebody here gonna make me get up . . . ." No one did, and it ran like a Hollywood movie, the new kid versus the gang. Yet this was not make believe; it was real, no one said, "Cut," and it ran on. And Bubba, unlike the new kid in the movies, was not a drifter, a loner—Bubba Smith could not, would not, live a life alone.

The phone became his friend, and he talked himself hoarse. He talked so much, he almost talked himself into marriage. She was black, fine, and ready. He had met her when he was at Michigan State, and her presence stayed with him. After the Colts' preseason game in Detroit, he gave her a ring.

When the Colts broke camp, he was the first to split. Decisions were not difficult for him, because he had no one to please but himself. He drove toward downtown Baltimore, and at the edge of the ghetto claimed the first building he saw. An apartment on Sutton Place was his. He called Beaver and invited him to stay with him, and his brother accepted. The Smiths of Sutton Place they were, and Bubba could relax a little. Beaver was happy, despite his being cut by Baltimore, and he bolstered his brother's spirit with memories of the good life, the family.

Smith was climbing up, out of the entombment of the Colt training camp atmosphere. His phone was busy, and he had a plan. His education at Michigan State had taught him a few things, especially about men and their women. The first preseason game was in Detroit, and as the team bus eased to a stop before the hotel, the plan began to go into effect. Four gorgeous, miniskirted twenty-year-old white females stood in the lobby entrance. As the team lowered themselves from the bus, their temperatures rose. The Colts circled those perfect creatures like vultures. Bubba had strategically placed himself in the back of the bus and was the last to debark. When he did, the young ladies swooned, ran to him, and began attending to him as though he were a Middle Eastern potentate out of a fairy tale: one took his valise; the other his attache case; yet another relieved him of his team bag; and the last helped him from the bus. "Check with ya'll later," he said, his index finger pointing toward heaven. Bubba missed the team meeting held an hour after arrival. He was fined one thousand dollars. The Colts won the game—number 78 rode the bench during the game—but lost the lobby, and every member of the team was looking at the bonus baby a bit differently.

Bubba's plan was still in force when the Baltimore Colts and Johnny Unitas—the team billing in every city—motored into St. Louis. Five stupendous black, brown, beige, tan and burple (blue-black that is) ladies stood demurely in front of the hotel. The Detroit action was repeated, this time in technicolor, and the beat went on and on until the team was back at their training home in Maryland. "No more women in the lobby or rooms," announced Shula at the end of a team meeting. Billy Ray Smith, who was on the first team and a spectacular athlete, stood and spoke. "If it's possible, I'd like to room with Bubba." Before the coach could reply, Bubba interjected, "I don't need you!"

"What is it, Bubba? Just trying to show a little team spirit!"

"Where were you my first weeks in camp?"

The master plan was working, yet Bubba began to accept that he would never have a real friend on this team. The politics had forced even the black players to ignore him. Only Lenny Moore and Jim Parker helped Bubba relax. During a game early in the season Jim and Lenny were sitting behind their standing teammates. Parker, who owned a liquor store in Maryland, had prepared himself for the game by taping tiny bottles of scotch to his shoulder pads. Every time Unitas completed a pass Jim and Lenny would empty the contents of one down their throats. Bubba, bored watching others play the game he loved, began to watch with amusement. After every bottle, pulled down as most people drink water, Lenny and Jim, in true drunken fashion, chorused, "Yan-ni-kin, yan-ni-kin, yan-ni-kin." Number 78 started laughing, and Coach Shula saw him. "What the fuck is going on?" he screamed with a megaphone wail, and both Moore and Parker flipped over in their chairs, screaming "Yan-ni-kin, yan-ni-kin, yan-ni-kin."

Unannounced, Smitty had flown to Michigan State for the Northwestern game. Tody was in pain and the team coach and doctor were treating his ankle injury as though it were cry-wolf time. Smitty had called ahead and made arrangements with a specialist who practiced in Ann Arbor and took his ailing son to him for an examination. The doctor said young Smith would never play football again and operated, boring a hole in his ankle and stretching a muscle from his calf down past the ankle to support it. The three-hour operation was successful, and three days later Sparky Lewis, El Toro's hurrah partner from Beaumont beckoned by telephone. "What is it, ferocious one, not strong enough to make the Christmas jamboree down here?" Carlton Moore, the hospital orderly, accepted twenty dollars at 5:00 the next morning, out, in a cab, and flying home, to party away the pain with people he could trust, by 8:20. Concerning the forecast for his career, Tody would only drop his head back on his huge shoulders and laugh like an athlete with plans.

The season was better than good for the Colts—they lost only two games—but the Los Angeles Rams took the conference, and Green Bay won the Super Bowl. The season was a time of adjustment for number 78. The Colts were playing him at tackle, and although he played it as ordered, end was his position. Off the field was where the action was: his fiancee was stripped of her ring after a few months of torrid romance. The end came when Bubba heard descriptive passages from Lem Barney and Mel Farr of their love lives. The name was never mentioned, but Smith was certain when he heard the quality of her scream parodied by both. Bubba was giving the best parties in Baltimore, and all of the beautiful women came through. The Colt team that had ignored him only heard about the action; none was invited.

All of the Baltimore niggahs loved him—he was the only player who had not escaped to the suburbs. Bubba would talk for hours with the real folks. One of the real folks was another rookie in another sport, Earl "the Pearl" Monroe. "The nearest thrill to playing myself was watching the Pearl play at the Civic Center." Earl Monroe was the Baltimore Bullets, and although most black athletes had always witnessed the finest hoopsters in the world, no one compared to the brilliance of Pearl. Bubba was at the game every chance he got, and when Pearl faked out the seven-foot Wilt the Stilt one game, Smith almost had a heart attack. "The only problem Pearl had was decorating his apartment—all the niggah had was fishnet and lights," Bubba says.

The other side of town, which felt a little like Beaumont, was the ghetto. Bubba was welcomed everywhere and anytime. One time he was rapping with some good people, and Little Melvin and his lady, Kathy, the black version of Bonnie and

Clyde, saw him and made him a bet. Little Melvin was the front for everythang, and his dress and wheels showed it with a definite flair. "You think you making some cash playin' ball?" he asked Bubba.

"I do all right."

"Well, I make in one day what you make in one year."

Smith removed his glasses so he could hear better.

"I'll bet you I could leave, say, sixty thousand open in a bag right here on the bar, and no one would touch it."

"Show me."

The bet was off, but the showboat was on. Little Melvin pulled out the cash, left the room, and nothing happened. Bubba, seeing all of those bills, thought about taking it himself, but after checking out his north, east, south, and west escape routes, and seeing them all filled with folks that resembled Little Melvin, all with their hands out of sight, Bubba ordered another Coke and relaxed. That was the kind of year 1967 was for one Smith. Looking, learning, and cherry cola.

January 1968: Michigan State had two Smiths on campus again. Bubba had six credits left before he could receive his degree. Returning student Smith had a new roommate and he seemed like a decent person, that is until the NFL Players Association called Smith to suggest he cut down on the dope. "The what?" asked Bubba. "I've never had any dope in my life." He hung up and sat there, a half-empty cherry cola before him, growing angrier by the second. He looked around the room, and his eyes stopped at his roommate's clothes closet. The door was snatched open, and behind the hanging jackets were two huge bags of marijuana, the bags the size of a boxers punching bag, filled to the brim. Bubba took them both out on Highway 496, opened them, and threw them to the winds. He drove back to the campus and went back to his room, where he found another small bag: Just when he had began to calm down, anger took him once again. He wasn't surprised by the bag, but he was upset that Tody had probably known about his roommate and had not told him, and he flushed the last of the supply down the toilet. His roommate got wind of what had happened and was never seen again on the MSU campus. The underground had it from the horse's mouth: if Bubba caught him his life would be at an end.

Tody was being called everything from a fake to a prima

donna by the coaches of Michigan State. He had continued to complain about his ankle months after it should have healed.

Off to Ann Arbor went Tody with his running partners, Sweet and Snap-down to Ann Arbor and the good doctor who had performed the surgery. After X rays and a thorough examination, the doctor, embarrassed professionally for the first time in his career, said he had left wire in Tody's ankle and would have to operate again. A telegram was sent to Duffy explaining the error.

When Tody returned, without the wire, he was given a full apology in front of the team.

At one minute past 6:00 PM, April 4, 1968, a rifle shot struck down Martin Luther King, Jr. By 7:00 he was dead. Another assassin had altered history, another hero gunned down by Satan.

Colt training camp, 1968. The sleek automobile squealed to a halt in front of the gates, and fans, reporters, and photographers ran to it, expecting the conservative-looking young man out of Michigan State. Out of the car emerged the new man: a five-inch Afro, sun-shade prescription glasses, love beads, and a brilliantly-colored dashiki. The fans' reaction? Ooh's and ah's, and the gingerbread giant loved it.

The writers, who knew the coach, had another response. "Shula going to make you cut that hair?" asked one. "What has hair got to do with playing football?" returned Bubba. "Nobody is gonna cut this hair!" The season's story was set—white coach, black militant. The time was ripe, and it was front-page news.

CHAPTER 7
My Time

THE SO-CALLED MILITANT had spent a thrilling June fulfilling a top-priority dream. It began as far back as he could remember, the reality of it beginning to being achieved after a team had gambled ten grand on Bubba joining the American Football League. The money was used to purchase a plot of land in the classy section of Beaumont. Ever since then he, Smitty, Tody, and Beaver pitched in by casually extracting architectural notions from Georgia. Operation Rita Baby was on. The information was dribbled to the architect, room by room, and the drawings were ready a day before the Notre Dame game. With the Colt signing five and a half months later, it was finished and paid for.

Like doves they flew to their original nest. Bubba and Smitty improvised her appearance, and Tody and Beav orchestrated the party and its needs. Everyone had huddled and scampered to their positions for the Super Bowl of surprises. Smitty was the center, driving; Bubba the quarterback, calling signals from the passenger seat; and Mama was the Queen of Roses, enjoying a ride through Beaumont.

After a half hour of "looking for somewhere to move," they happened to find themselves on Blossom Street. The car slowed as it had a half dozen times before, and Georgia found herself calculating the value of every house. "Sweethearts, this is too expensive around here. Shouldn't we try another neighborhood? There's a house over on Clifford Street that I've been . . ." Smitty had turned into the driveway of the freshly built house and stopped. Georgia, a stickler for law and order, began chirping like a parakeet, asking Smitty, "Sweetheart, wouldn't it be best if we backed out of these people's driveway—they may get angry." By the time she had finished, Bubba was out of the car and opening her door. "Hey, Mama, let's just take a look at how the rich people live. Okay?" Miss Georgia was beside herself, getting more nervous by the second. She knew the penalty for trespassing, and if a patrol car came by, well, we all know what she would do.

Smitty and Bubba were performing brilliantly—not since *Mission: Impossible* had such a delicate operation been attempted. The center snapped the look to the quarterback, and like a bell tolling in the soft twilight of Beaumont, Bubba's long, delicate hand was extended, a key hanging from his middle finger. "It's yours, Mother!" A true Bubbaism—why say more? Simple, loving, and to the point.

The lights flashed on, the flashbulbs popped, the music played "Music, Maestro, Please," and Smitty and his bride of twenty-seven years danced to the rhythmic clapping of their friends and neighbors. Her moment was the family's moment, and happy tears were gliding down Mama's cheeks as her man, Doll, swept her over, around, and beyond their lawn.

An ageless Moses leaned against a willow tree and grinned, nodding his silver head to the tempo.

No one was grinning in Westminster, Maryland. Shula called a private meeting with his number 78. The chief topic was Bubba's transformation from Clark "Dark" Kent to what Rap Brown had hoped he looked like. "My hair and wardrobe have nothing to do with my playing," Bubba said. "Anything asked of me on the field, I'll do." Shula said something about avoiding trouble with the press. "If you stop shouting at me, making me a scapegoat in front of the team, like you did last season, we can avoid a lotta trouble," Bubba retorted. They attempted to start the season on a good foot.

Press time, and the camera's flashing reminded Bubba of a Juneteenth celebration in Texas. He sat on his helmet, away from the commotion, and awaited the politics. He hoped he would remain cool. Baltimore wanted the ghost of the great Big Daddy Lipscomb, but he was uniquely Charles Aaron "Bubba"

Smith. He kept saying to himself, "Yan-ni-kin, yan-ni-kin, yan-ni-kin," the Moore-Parker drunken slogan, and it made him smile. One of the assistants walked over and asked him to pose with the starting defensive line. "Why?" he asked. "Shula said so!" was the reply. "I'm not start——" Here he was, waiting for the politics to start, and things were reversed—he was on the good end of a screwing. A two-year player, Roy Hilton, had been the first-team end, but there was Hilton, standing alone near the cage. Bubba had wanted to work for it, to beat his competition. As he rose, he warned them secretly, If you're handing it to me, you'll never get it back. It was enough of a challenge, he thought, to make him work. His father had reiterated the magic phrase, *You must be twice as good,* when he was home. He would be better than that.

Because of his never-ending entertaining during his boring rookie year, the owners of his apartment on Sutton Place had politely asked him not to return in 1968. With the Temptations rocking his brand-new dark-brown Cadillac convertible, he found himself driving to a townhouse. Motoring past rows and rows of red-brick houses all alike, all fronted by a white stoop. The two-story was near Morgan State College, on Beaumont Street. His new home, and he would be a good, clean-living man and work at his profession in a thoroughly professional way.

    A telephone call came three days later while number 78 was going through his drills. As soon as he received the message, he asked the Baltimore trainer for a huge supply of vitamins. It was an old friend from Michigan State. After he had finished explaining to Bubba why his ball team had cut him so early in the season, Bubba dropped to his knees, laughing, the phone still in his hand. The guy was good—it was no shock, but losing a career because of it was pushing it a bit. He had a sleeping problem, a serious one, which his team had been unable to deal with, no matter how good he was at his trade. It was impossible for him to sleep without a lady. No joke, no game, no play; that's merely how he functioned. Bubba invited him over for the weekend on his way home to Birmingham, Michigan.

    When a great-looking guy, suave and white, arrived at Beaumont Street, he had that look in his blue eyes. There were two problems: Bubba had to go to practice; and he didn't know any ladies of the guy's race. He swallowed a laugh when Bubba said that, and they made a deal. He would drive Bubba to practice, take the car, and find a Sominex for himself.

Roy Hilton, whom Bubba had replaced on the first team, drove him home after practice that afternoon. When they arrived at Beaumont Street, all they could hear was the get-down sounds of James Brown pleading. Bubba thanked Roy for the transportation and was about to book when Hilton asked, droolingly, "Don't ya want me to come in?" Bubba replied characteristically, "No," and bounded the stairwell. Once in, a quartet of the finest black damsels to be seen in the Atlantic states sat, stood, and slouched in Bubba's living room. "Hi, how ya doing?" Bubba said cheerily to the ladies and wagged a come-here finger at his guest, who was calmly rapping away.

Man to man they conferred in the bedroom. "Well, I thought since you've been so nice to me—I brought along two for you." He was deadly serious.

The season, the football season that is, was also adventurous. Number 78 had his position, his confidence, and his fans yelling, "Kill, Bubba, kill!" He took on more and more responsibility, though a fractured wrist during a preseason game slowed him. His left wrist was caught under a pileup. The Caine sisters, Nova and Xyla, soothed the pain, while the taped binding held it firm.

A player named Bob Brown, nicknamed Boomer, was his first opponent of the season. The last time Bubba had seen him play, Boomer was with the Philadelphia Eagles. Bubba was on the bench, and the rookie watched as the veteran Colt line looked and acted scared. They had every right to be scared, because Boomer was the toughest lineman 78 had ever seen play the game. The first play showed that his own fear was right on. Boomer knocked Bubba on his ass. It had never happened before. And, worse, Brown's red eyes looked squarely into Smith's soul as he aimed at the fallen Colt and speared him with a head-first, diving tackle. Bubba promised himself that if it took his entire professional life, Bob Brown would belong to him.

The National Football League belonged to the Colts that year; their only loss came against Cleveland. Twelve teams fell to the powerhouse led by Johnny Unitas, among the most talented quarterbacks ever to play the game. In one game Johnny U proved his mettle to Bubba. "We were playing the

Bears. They hit him, and after they hit him, they gave him the ghetto flip. [The tackler takes the player, turns him upside down, and spears him head-first into the ground.] I thought his neck was broken, but he got up, brushed himself off, went back to the huddle, and called the same play. When the ball was snapped, the same tackler came through the line, and Johnny U hit him right in the face with the ball. Broke his nose."

Johnny U, however, had been injured, and Earl Morrall was the quarterback when the team finished the season against the Rams. Bob Brown, who had embarrassed Bubba in the season's first game, faced him again, this time on Boomer's turf, the Los Angeles Coliseum. Both had watched the films made during the season and had noticed each other's improvement. Bubba, who despite his image used a great deal more cunning than force, had reconciled himself to beating Bob Brown with speed rather than might. What number 78 had to do was get around Boomer and sack Roman Gabriel. He had tried to get through Boomer—around him was a touch easier. Mr. Gabriel paid dearly that afternoon, and Bubba had beaten Boomer the only way an intelligent player could. He remained a fan of Mr. Brown; and asked about Bubba later, Brown told Larry Harris of *Quarterback* magazine, "I guess you people of the press will never know how good Bubba Smith is until you put on a uniform and get out there and play him. I can tell you without any hesitation that I voted for him on the players' all-pro team. He is a load, and you can quote me."

The final game, which the Colts had to win to make the cherished Super Bowl and a quick fifteen thousand dollars, was against the Cleveland Browns and the National Football League's leading rusher, Leroy Kelly. Eighty-four thousand people in Cleveland's Municipal Stadium watched 78 sack quarterback Bill Nelson five times, block three field goal attempts, and perform seven unassisted tackles. By the fourth quarter the score was 24–0.

Attempting to block a pass in the final quarter, Bubba turned in midair to watch its flight and was hit violently from behind. Escorted from the field, he received a standing ovation from the fans of the opposing team. His leg was seriously sprained; he thanked God it wasn't broken.

Larry Kelly had been held to twenty-seven yards, and the Baltimore Colts were in Super Bowl III.

A mob at Friendship International Airport awaited their triumphant heroes. Bubba, on crutches, should have used a later flight, but the Baltimore fans probably would have waited for him until dawn. The police tried their best, but the fans' enthusiasm swamped both the cops and Bubba. Bob "Boomer" Brown would have smiled when number 78 found himself under the mob. A score of Baltimore's finest was sent to escort the crippled Colt through the multitude, who yelled, "Kill, Bubba, kill!" The words came near to having another meaning that evening.

B. Smith needed a quiet night, yet when he arrived at his Beaumont Street home, a party was in full swing. He asked everyone to leave, after thanking them for coming. The night ended as well the weekend visit of his MSU friend—after five months Bubba was exhausted in more ways than one.

Santa Barbara, California, January 2, 1969: Jimmy "the Greek" Snyder, the Las Vegas oddsmaker who set the nation's betting line on everything from the Triple Crown to national elections, listed the Baltimore Colts as eighteen-point favorites.

Before the game Joe Willie Namath, the Jets quarterback, surprised even his own teammates when he committed the cardinal sin in sports. He evaluated an opponent in less than flattering terms for the public. Earl Morrall, he said, who would be quarterbacking the Colts, was not very good. He also said, "We are going to win on Sunday, I guarantee you." Joe Namath was as prototypical a football player as Muhammad Ali was a boxer. Bubba Smith, his leg in a cast, when it wasn't in a whirlpool, said, "Joe is one of the finest quarterbacks I've ever seen, next to *Johnny Unitas,* and what he's doing now is a wonderful gimmick. Joe really has nothing to lose. If he wins, he's a fortune teller: if he loses, it was a beautiful try."

The New York Jets arrived at Fort Lauderdale January 3. They used the Galt Ocean Mile Motel for lodging and Fort Lauderdale Stadium for practice sessions. January 5 the Baltimore Colts arrived and quartered themselves at the Statler-Hilton Hotel and used the facilities of St. Andrew's Boys School in Boca Raton for practice.

The teams hoorrahed each other, led by Lou Michaels of the Colts and the young man from Beaver Falls, Pennsylvania, christened Joseph Alexander Namath. He had changed his name when he played at Alabama—a political gesture that endeared him to the Billy Rays and the Jimmy Johns, the southern-borns who were his teammates. So it was now Joe Willie who said, "We're going to kick hell out of your team."

"Suppose we kick hell out of you," said Michaels. "Then what will you do, Namath?"

"I'll tell you what I'll do. I'll sit down right in the middle of the field, and I'll cry."

Tending to their injuries, both Bubba and Johnny Unitas watched Namath on film. One move gave Bubba hope for a few sacks. "Willie Boy uses a ten-yard drop," he said, describing the distance the quarterback fell back after the center had snapped the ball. With that much room, Bubba thought, he should be an open target—if my wheels are straight. He wore a boat, a temporary rubber boot, from his groin to his foot, and it frustrated the hell out of him.

Both teams of athletes had sharpened their moves and minds, gearing up to kill, preparing for the biggest show in America, the Super Bowl. Yet they were commanded, like children, to meet the media to answer questions like "How do you feel about the Super Bowl?" "Do you sleep well?" "Do you take dope?" "Do you like women?" Of course there were those reporters professional enough to have prepared themselves with a working knowledge of the game—those that talked to players as though they were adults—but in 1969 they were rare. A sadder problem was those first-year players who, enjoying the attention, began to change to suit the reporter. One niggah changed his age, birth place, college, and marital status depending on who the reporter was.

Bubba's leg cast was removed. John Mackey, one of the greatest ends to play the game, wanted to practice live for timing. Live meant all-out hitting at game intensity. Bubba was worried about the extent of his injury, but there was no way of telling until it was tested. At the end of the first day he discovered that his ankle, although sore, held strong. John and Bub gutted up and went live for the next three practice days—until both were bleeding.

Bubba felt the tension growing in others. The loudest, wrongest, and lowest dudes were now low-key. Some sent for female companionship until their wives arrived—Bubba's ladies were bumping into each other in the corridors—until it was time for discipline. Coach Shula imposed a bed check three days before the game.

That morning arrived on schedule. The buses were late. Imagine that—a multimillion-dollar event, and the buses were late. A nervous group of battle-ready athletes shifted from foot to foot, waiting for a bus. When the buses did arrive, Bubba, as always, was the last to get on, and he stood in the stairwell across from the driver. Jets' buses, he noticed, were ahead of the Colts'. "Why are the Jets in front?" he asked the driver. "They left first" was his sage reply, but it didn't satisfy Bubba. "The National League should be first—we're the senior league." His mind raced to comprehend the symbolism of the moment.

The usual bullshit and hoorrah that is the routine of team bus rides was absent; most of the men were meditating. The mood was excellent for a championship team. Three times during the twelve-game winning season had they been this intense before a game—the Kansas City preseason game, the Rams game, and the final game in Cleveland. The Colts had won them all.

It was hope-to-die business when the bus stopped in front of the Orange Bowl. The team moved out quietly, and 78 headed straight for the locker room. His ankles were taped twice, and he put on pads, leggings, pants, and tee shirt and went to sleep on the floor for twenty minutes.

When he awoke, he looked for the key men on the team. Mike Curtis understood his unarticulated question and nodded yes. Rick Volk gave him the thumbs-up victory signal. He walked over to John Mackey. "Just give me a little rest between our times on the field, and we'll whip the hell out of them." Mackey, the offensive leader, replied, "They'll be up!" The machine called the Baltimore Colts was ready for action.

The reigning king of football, J. U., John Unitas, with his bristle haircut and Henry Fonda squareness, was injured but ready to back up his replacement, Earl Morrall. That J. U. was in the locker room and suited up, Bubba thought, assured the outcome of the game. John was as predictable as the daylight and appeared as relaxed as if he were at a boy scout picnic. Nothing had changed, from the first day of training camp, about Johnny Unitas.

There were those players who prayed; those who hit the lockers with taped fists; those who vomited. Some wrote letters like soldiers before battle, and there was Bubba Smith, who charged and recharged his soul until he felt he could kill with precision.

This Colt team had to play well, not over their heads, merely consistently. The team prayed in unison, and coach Shula spoke. "Don't wait for them to lose it. We've got to win it ourselves."

It was time to enter the arena, and out they went, into the

screaming circus. As much a part of that wonderful circus as the clowns, animals, and sideshows, Bubba was not a freak but the ringmaster who had trained himself all of his life to fill center stage. In the audience was the man who had led him to center stage and the woman who had taught him about caring, his mother and father.

As the national anthem ended— "and the home of the brave!"—"The roar of the fans cheered on my neurotic need for victory. Out jogged Lenny Lyles, our cocaptain and their captain, Johnny Sample. I saw Sample's mouth move when the referee signaled he had won the toss. When Lenny returned, I asked him what Sample had said: 'The first one goes to us, sucker!'

"Shula had told us, as was his custom, what the first four offensive plays would be. The first was the 36 trap play, the play that Mackey and I had bled over. Morrall called it, and Mackey busted Gary Philburn, the middle linebacker, and the outside linebacker with his brute force. My left leg remembered the pain my eyes were witnessing. The hole in the Jet line opened as wide as a team bus. Our running back, Tom Matte, took off. My fist was in air, and I found myself jumping with Matte's every step. The same Jet linebacker who had been flattened by Mackey leaped to his feet, ran, and caught Matte on the twenty-five-yard line. No one could believe he had been stopped short of the end zone. The how-could-it-have-happened looks swept through the team. There was no answer, only questioning looks. Three plays and zero yardage later, in went the field goal team—and we missed.

"The sad result of our first series of plays stayed with us," Bubba says, "we had no time to focus on what had gone down. It was defense time, my time."

Bubba had Dave Herman to contend with. At six feet two inches, two hundred fifty-five pounds he was a tremendous, hustling lineman, a Michigan State Spartan, but too small to worry 78. After their first series, though, the Jet game plan seemed to say that Bubba would have a long day—three blockers on him, and all the plays were called to run at the Colts' left.

The Jets lined up again, and Namath handed off to their great running back, Matt Snell. Snell was running a swing play, and Rick Volk attempted a head-first dive at him. A sickening meeting of the minds. Rick did not get up, and the stretchers took him off the field.

The first half was a series of fumbles, but Namath began to

move the Jets, while Morrall was having problems finding anyone to pass to. "All I could do," Bubba recalls, "was find the right time to get past Herman, Boozer, and Snell and get to Joe. On one play Namath went back to throw, Dave missed me, and I was dead on toward Joe Willie. The choice was to stumble and end his career by destroying his already crippled knee or hit him high and hold him. If it was a Tarkenton, I would have sent him to the hospital, but I chose to let Namath live. Even though Namath was turning into a quarterback machine, I couldn't cripple him."

It was the white-uniformed Jets, 7, and the blue-shirted Colts, 0, at the half. Only three plays had been directed at number 78, just to keep him honest. The 36 trap play that had worked to perfection was never used again. The final play of the half, the flea flicker, was a sound call, but it broadcast to the Jets that the Colts had panicked. "I ran into the locker room," Bubba says. "'Place me in the middle on defense so I can get into the flow of the game!' They looked at me blankly and rejected the idea. I went to our defensive coach, and asked, 'What's happening to us?' The thorough professional refused to discuss the offensive team's problems; he only reviewed the defense. While he spoke, everyone was looking past him, to Johnny Unitas, who appeared as though he were still at that scout picnic and was getting bored. He seemed to be waiting for the scout master's call; so was the team.

"The thought of J. U. entering the game buoyed me, and I felt my confidence ooze back. 'What are we worried about—we're only down by seven,' I said to the group around me. They gave me a give-me-a-break look."

Shula was screaming, as usual, and his emotions bounced off the locker room walls. "Stupid mistakes . . . Stopping ourselves . . . They're believing in themselves, believing they're better than we are." He was never more right. Not one adjustment had been made to prevent a repetition of the first half, yet Bubba had new faith. "We were out on the field again, and I heard a distant chant that took me back a few years. I heard, 'Kill, Bubba, kill!' And I just knew that Mama had something to do with that."

The kick-off was in the air, and the Colts took over on the thirty-yard line. The first play from scrimmage saw Tom Matte fumble. The Jets recovered, and after three plays the defense had held, only to see the Jets kick a field goal. Ten—zip, Jets.

On the next series came the moment that caused migraines

throughout Coltsville, USA. Earl Morrall had Johnny Orr standing in the end zone, alone. Orr was waving furiously to Morrall, but Earl never looked at him, never glanced at his primary receiver. He threw at Jimmy Hill with five Jets surrounding him. The pass was intercepted.

Two more Jet field goals brought the score to 16–0, and the underdogs were leading what had been called "the best team in football. Unitas was brought in to replace Earl, and he was cold. He did produce Baltimore's only touchdown, but it came too late, and the game ended, 16–7. Joe Willie, deservedly, was honored as the most valuable player.

The gun went off, signaling the end of the game. "I walked behind the rest of the team," Bubba remembers. "It was clearly the worst game the team had played since I had become a Colt. Not that we hadn't lost by bigger scores, but those games couldn't have been won. This one, this championship—there was not one excuse. We lost it."

Back in the same locker room that had smelled of victory only hours before, Bubba sat on his stool as the team prayer was said and thought, Did I give everything that I could have? He went through the game play by play, in his mind, and when he had finished, almost everyone had showered, dressed, and left. "I walked like an eighty-year-old to the shower, placed my hand on the faucet, and turned it on full," Bubba said, "The ice-cold water hit me like a storm, and I screamed, 'I don't believe this stupid shit!' I never expected a reply, and I don't believe I received one.

"Mama and Daddy were in the lounge with Beaver. 'Sweetheart, it's going to be all right,' said ever-faithful Mama. Coach Smith had another thought: 'You were out-coached, son!' Beaver stared through me. 'It's over, Bub—don't hold onto it.'"

After the game Rick Volk, the victim of the collision with the human tank, Matt Snell, was found lying in the bathroom, vomiting, his body shaking with convulsions, swallowing his tongue. Fortunately Dr. Norman Freeman, the team physician was near, and he used a ballpoint pen to free Volk's tongue. At Holy Cross Hospital Volk regained consciousness, looked at his wife, and asked, "Who won?"

Bubba Smith never lost consciousness—he wished he had, and he knew who had lost. He was dry, bone-drained with the bitterness of defeat. Nevertheless he escorted his best girl,

Georgia Smith, to the party at the home of Carroll Rosenbloom, twenty minutes from Fort Lauderdale, near the beach.

A Colt— blue-and-white tent had been raised for the occasion on the vast Rosenbloom lawn. There were Rosenbloom waiters and Rosenbloom bartenders, even a Rosenbloom dance band. Only sixty hope-to-die Colt folks were present of the two hundred or more invited. The others were probably partying with Namath; nobody likes a loser, Bubba thought, a thought voiced bluntly of course to all present.

His absolutely truthful style was answered in Rosenbloom fashion: a glass of the bubbly was handed to him. The champagne spilled a bit, running gracefully down and over the Colt horseshoe cut in the glass. Bubba was learning more and more about white folks, but the hoopla celebration at this party flabbergasted him, so much so that he quickly downed three glasses. Georgia, correct for any occasion, playing the role of mother of a team star on the surface, was worried sick about her depressed baby on the real side. She remarked on his drinking—it was the first time she had seen him take one drink much less three. And it was only the second time in his life he had ever had anything to drink. The first, a disaster, was at a Michigan State frat dance. He found himself flat on his Peter Prep face swearing never again, a promise the day had erased.

Bubba finished his cigarette and the remnants of his third drink and decided to teach class. "I'll be right back," he mumbled. "For the glory of Charlton Pollard and Michigan State, two teams with integrity . . . ." With those words he rose like a cobra from his chair. His six feet eight inches were aimed at the dance floor. A samba was playing, and many of his teammates were attempting to dance. He moved toward his prey in classic John Wayne fashion, adding a touch of color of course and maneuvered himself from the lawn the foot up to the dance floor. Tom Matte was the target for tonight. He reached for him, as one would for a sack of flour, and lifted the two-hundred-pound-plus athlete over his five-inch Afro, and heaved him into the empty tables on the lawn.

Mama Smith was next to him in a flash and calmly escorted him out of the party. She understood the problem—her sweetheart was not a loser and refused to celebrate defeat. When they were past the Rosenbloom iron gate, she asked sweetly, "What did you expect?" He was motioning for a taxi as he answered her simple question. "Mama, I have no idea, I guess anything but what I saw!" He decided to send her home. He kissed her lovingly, paid the driver, and off she went into the Florida night. Another cab pulled in front of him, and he piled himself in, asking the driver to take the long beach route to the hotel. "I need to cool my head down."

The trip was silent except for the buzz in Bubba's brain. A voice from the driver's seat interrupted. The lilting African-Irish sound was followed by an ebony face gleaming with an ear-to-ear gold-toothed grin. The identification card on the dashboard read CLIFFORD EMMANUEL LOCKLEY. There was no question but that he was from the West Indies, mon. "You're simply spectacular at wot you do, mon!" he shouted. A stranger gushing compliments eased Bubba's blue mood. "My God, mon, you are a supreme thespian, an actor of the highest caliber."

Bubba thought, This niggah thinks I'm Marlon Brando. "Who do you think I am?" he asked. The cab stopped for a red light, and Clifford turned to his passenger. "Mon, you are the one, the only Bubber Smith, the footballer." The cab got the green, and the chattering driver continued, "My good mon, my wife, my woman, my girlfriend, my mother, and my three chirren give their humble thanks to you. All of our bills have been paid. Oh Christ, Christmas has come to the meek!"

Bubba slowly began, "Hey man, now hold on . . . what are you . . . er———"

"It was a gift, mon. Saturday at Hialeah race track—that's when I heard the word."

"What has Hialeah and your family have to do with——"

"I pick up this mon who turn out to be the famous East Coast Eddie. He won a sizeable amount and was feeling luxurious—that is when he put the bee in my ear!"

"Niggah, what has all this got to do with me?" Bubba exploded.

"The Bet!" the surprised Clifford replied. He was still smiling. "You just left his house, mon. Rosenbloom, the bet. The Rosenbloom bet. Come on now, all of the multicash folks knew. The Holy Ghost smiled upon me on Saturday!"

"I'm still waiting."

"East Coast say it was a cool million on the Jets to win!" When he reached the hotel, Bubba rushed to his suite, unlocked the door and walked directly out onto the balcony and yelled his black Texas yell: "Please, God, make it a lie!"

America, 1969: Richard Nixon becomes President of the

United States; James Earl Ray and Sirhan B. Sirhan are in prison, and Martin Luther King, Jr., and Robert Kennedy are dead; and the Manson Family brutally murders six in California. America leaps to the moon on Apollo 11, and New York continues to dominate Baltimore, in baseball this time.

The Colts sleepwalked through their season, winning eight and losing five, and Bubba Smith moved to new quarters. The Twin Towers on Charles Street became his home. His search for a true friend, besides his family, ended when he met Stanley Cohen. And Shula versus Smith continued. "We expected him to make even more improvement after that fine '68 season," said coach Shula. "We expected him to put himself right up there in a class with Carl Eller and Deacon Jones, the best defensive ends in the game. Unfortunately he didn't improve that way, but then again there were a lot of people on our club, not only Bubba, who didn't improve." Replied Mr. Smith, "Shula wants me to be someone else. He dreams of a combination Marchetti–Big Daddy Lipscomb.... Perhaps if he tried to understand Bubba Smith and his development, things might run smoother."

There was sunshine, though, in Lawrence Edward "Tody" Smith's pocket. He had found peace, for a moment. Like everything valuable it took teamwork, and young Smith had found his team and was allowed to work in Southern California.

A man named Willie Brown, an assistant coach at USC, had made the difference when Tody chose to transfer. When he had arrived at the LA airport, Willie's face had been the only face that resembled his, and Brown had good manners and showed a certain respect for Tody. And when Tody saw the team practice and felt the power of the USC front line, he was flabbergasted with the talent. The players confessed to him that the coach was fair—it was up to Tody whether he played on the first team; no politics this trip. Under the guidance of coach John McKay and with the fortune of good health, he was now the rage of Los Angeles.

Bubba and Tody had talked every other day by telephone; now United Airlines was making it in person. When Charles Aaron disengaged his seat belt, said so long to his acquaintances in first class—they all talked to him now—winked at the stewardess, and strode into the terminal, he could feel the relaxation of the city. The snow of Baltimore was replaced by the sun of LA.

El Toro stood there in his Smith stance, his costume bright as a peacock's plumage—six feet six inches of modern fashion smiling the smile of a winner. His chapeau, resembling those worn by the Three Musketeers, was tilted just right over his brow, and he wore a bossa nova shirt (a skin tight body shirt with tapered, ballooning sleeves), form-fitting bell-bottoms that flared just below the knee, and of course rainbow-colored shoes.

The style king was accompanied by his best friend, Willard "Bubba" Scott, whom Tody had nicknamed Freeze. Tody didn't want Freeze to be called Little Bubba and, more important, his partner loved, cherished, and revered chocolate Frosty Freeze ice cream. Freeze was a distant cousin of the Smiths, by way of his Nacogdoches-born father. These two, along with Jimmy Gunn, Al Cowlings, and Charles Weaver, made up the cast of characters known as the Wild Bunch, the most talented, meanest, and wildest defensive quartet ever to play collegiate football. The name of course was inspired by the title of an unusually violent film.

On Lawrence Edward's arm was a lady, his lady, Tate Maretha Washington. She was looking at her man like there was no other, and of course Tody agreed. They had met on campus. Miss Washington, nicknamed Tango or Little Squaw, depending on Tody's needs, had swished herself past the Texan one smoggy California day. When student Smith had cleared his eyes, having strained them while inspecting the new crop of coeds, he followed her incredible rhythmic motion until he couldn't take anymore. Using his best Clark Gable voice, he whispered, "Honestly, my dear, you're gonna twist yo' butt off." That was three months before. There wasn't a ring—Bubba's was busy—but you could tell that all five feet six, one hundred twenty pounds of her fine brown frame belonged to El Toro.

Bubba felt at home. Home is where the heart is, and his heart belonged to his family. Despite Tody's costume, he was still part of the family. Bub became an instant fan of the Wild Bunch and Tango.

There was something that Tody had achieved that Bubba hadn't, an All-American team honor that El Toro possessed: *Playboy* Magazine All-American. He chose that topic to begin conversation on the way into town.

The 1968 Heisman Trophy winner, O. J. Simpson, renewed his acquaintanceship with Bubba that week, and they spearheaded the rah-rah group supporting the team. USC had come from behind to beat Stanford, Georgia Tech, California, and Washington, and now it was UCLA's turn. It was the Wild Bunch versus the Quiet Bunch for the national and city championship—LA's famous rivals, USC versus UCLA, and Tody Smith loved the drama. Both teams were unbeaten; both had won eight, tied one. Tommy Protho, the UCLA coach, called it his best team, and they were favored by two points. Dennis Dummit, who had passed for two thousand yards was the quarterback.

UCLA led 6–0 in the first quarter. Charley Weaver knocked down the attempt at a two-point pass conversion, and for the next fifty-four minutes the Wild Bunch dominated the game. When Al Cowlings tackled Mickey Curatin he asked him, "Did you forget that this game was on national TV?" Tody almost decapitated a UCLA back, and after the play he pointed a finger at him and said, "There isn't a lady in those stands that you can get now, sucker."

USC scored on a thirteen-yard run by Clarence Davis, and Ayala's conversion gave USC a 7–6 half-time lead. With only five minutes remaining in the game, Dummit connected on a fifty-seven-yard pass, and with three minutes left UCLA scored a touchdown. The Wild Bunch prevented the pass conversion. Then USC quarterback Jimmy Jones laid the ball up, and Sam Dickerson made a tremendous catch and a touchdown. Ayala converted, and USC won, 14–12.

"I checked my heart," said John McKay, the coaching genius of USC, "and I don't have one." "He has quite a heart, one of the purest I've ever been close to," said Tody Smith, a very happy member of the wildest bunch of football players America had ever seen.

The Bunch went on to capture the Rose Bowl, beating Michigan, 16–3, when Bobby Chandler caught a Jimmy Jones pass and ran the remaining twenty yards for the winning score. The Smiths were champs, a position they had gotten used to but never took for granted.

Tody, the style influence of the family, talked Bubba into going Mod that year—imagine two giants in platform-heeled shoes. One partying night in a posh Beverly Hills disco, characteristically called the Candy Store, the now seven-foot Smith, with heels, almost broke his Super Bowl ankle while dancing. He did meet two people he dug, an exotically beautiful woman named Verna, soon adorned with his trusty diamond ring, and an actor, the first he had met he could relate to. The dude's name was James Caan, Michigan State graduate, and they talked about school days, sports, and of course females. While they were in deep discussion, "Caan kept looking away. I began thinking, Damn, I must be getting a little boring," says Smith. "James says 'Hold on a minute,' and walked a few steps away, cocked his fist, and hit this sucker in the mouth. He then began stomping him ghetto style." Bubba continues, "This was the first Hollywood dude who was legit. The tough little movie star—white boy was a man."

Smith was beginning to feel loose when the news came. He had to get back and work himself into the best shape of his life. The news handed to him hot off the wire by a Los Angeles reporter: Shula was out, owner Carroll Rosenbloom had put the team into the American Conference of the National Football League in exchange for three million dollars. Don Shula had gone to become head coach of the Miami Dolphins, and number 78 left Tody Town, or T.S. Country, to become head man of his team. He commented boarding his flight to the Maryland snow, "Fine, maybe we'll get a coach now who'll treat us like human beings instead of dogs."

Don McCafferty, a Colt assistant, a warm man, became the new coach. John Sandusky, the defensive line coach, called number 78 in for a conference. Respect grew, almost immediately, when Sandusky showed Smith films of his performance. They spoke easily, and in two hours Bubba learned something about football. He was ecstatic. "John changed my stance," he recalls. "My butt was either too high or too low; I'd take precious time to drop or lift it before I charged; I needed a happy medium. It was the first time since Hank Bullough or my father had talked with me that I learned something." Sandusky was so sharp in his knowledge of football that Bubba went home and began thinking of questions to ask him, to test his overall understanding of the game. "I began to have fun again," he says. "The man cared about me, and even more important he cared about the sport that was paying for his living.... We looked at game films of the great players Gino Marchetti, Deacon Jones, and Carl Eller. Gino took unbelievable risks; Deacon was precise; and Eller never stopped hustling. The conversations became so detailed that I learned to watch the veins on the opposing players' hands. If the veins were poppin', it meant rush usually. If they were relaxed, it was a pass play. How to look at down and distance. Reading the play before it happened. I had always had technique, but working with John, it crystallized.

"The Colt training camp was a treat. I couldn't wait to get there. Coach McCafferty had the identical vocal tone as Smitty, and it stayed that way, unless you weren't hustling at all!" says a beaming Smith. "He even played poker with the team.

"Sandusky psyched me into more hustle than even I expected. Sprints after an all-day practice was a definite no for me, but John knew how to motivate me. He knew I was a leader, and he would casually walk over to me and say, 'Bub, I want you to head up these sets of sprints.' I had to do it, my ego had painted me into a corner, but I was in the best shape of my life."

The Colts broke their necks for Coach McCafferty that 1970 season. It wasn't a roll-through, but they won eleven of fourteen. The most important game was against the Jets and Joe Willie. Bubba remembers one play very well. "I had moved an inch offside. I was fired up for a blitz on Joe [Namath had thrown sixty-two passes], and I couldn't stop myself. I hollered at him, trying to warn him, 'Stop!' I could easily have crippled him for life. Joe stopped, and I cradled him. Returning to the huddle, Joe Foley, a Jet lineman, hit me on the back of the head. I was knocked off balance but caught myself and went after Foley. The Jet bench yelled duck, and I missed him. The next four plays I went after him and only him—he'll never forget it."

The next time the teams met, a fluke accident occurred. Bubba respected Joe Willie. "He was straight out, man," says Bubba, remembering the injury to his friend. Number 78 had broken through the line and was about to crush Namath. As he charged, he knew that if he hit Namath with the speed he was traveling, Joe's career would come to an end that day. He yelled to Joe, "Jump!" Namath knew the play was hopeless, but he jumped the wrong way, into Bubba, and his hand hit Bub's helmet with a resounding crack. Willie Joe's hand was broken, and Bubba was unhappy for his friend for a week. He had even gone to the Jet locker room after the game to see how Namath was. Joe Willie understood what had happened and thanked him for his mercy.

The Colts showed no mercy for the rest of the season and were in the Super Bowl again. They worked out in subfreezing weather for the game, then flew to Miami. For luck the team changed airlines, accommodations, and practice field, all different from the last time they had made this trip.

The Dallas Cowboys—ten wins, four defeats—would be the

Colts' rival, the Cowboys having defeated the San Francisco 49ers, 17–10, for their title. It was Don McCafferty, in his first year as coach, against Tom Landry, "a student of football technology as Wernher von Braun is a student of aerospace technology," reported *The New York Times*. Although domestic problems plagued veteran quarterback John Unitas, he was healthy and ready this time around. Landry had alternated Roger Staubach, then in his second year, with his veteran, Craig Morton, during the season, but Morton was selected to start. Two rookies would oppose each other in the running game—Duane Thomas for the Cowboys and Norm Bulaich for the Colts. And Dallas was a one-point favorite in Vegas.

The Super Bowl V goofs list turned out to be the highlight of the game. Johnny Unitas threw an interception to Dallas linebacker Chuck Howley seven minutes after the game began. The Cowboys punted after three plays. Ron Gardin, the Baltimore safety, fumbled it. Cliff Harris recovered for Dallas. Craig Morton, taking over on the Colts' nine-yard line, couldn't score. Mike Clark kicked a field goal.

After moving the ball to the Colts' seven, thanks to Bob Hayes' sensational catch, Morton single-handedly moved the Cowboys in the wrong direction by throwing to an ineligible receiver, thus earning a fifteen-yard penalty, then failing to see Duane Thomas standing alone, nothing but goal posts around him. The Cowboys settled for Clark's second field goal, and the score was 6–0 Dallas.

On a Colt third down Unitas threw a pass intended for Eddie Hinton that flew far over his head. Hinton jumped and deflected the ball toward Cowboy Mel Renfro. Renfro could not hold it, and it finally settled in the arms of John Mackey, Colt tight end, who took it seventy-five yards for a touchdown. Score, 6–6. Jim O'Brien, the Colts' rookie kicker, had his extra point blocked by Mark Washington.

Unitas, after getting the ball back following a Dallas punt, fumbled, and Dallas recovered on the Baltimore twenty-eight-yard line. Dallas scored— Morton was finally able to see Duane Thomas.

Unitas was forced out of the game by a tackle by George Andrie and Earl Morrall, the scapegoat for Baltimore's 1969 loss, was his replacement. Morrall began well but couldn't score after being on the Dallas two-yard line for three plays.

After the half Jim Duncan of the Colts fumbled the kickoff, and Dallas recovered. A few minutes later Duncan vindicated himself. Duane Thomas fumbled on the one-yard line, and Duncan fell on it, but rookie kicker O'Brien missed again.

An Earl Morrall pass was intercepted—the sixth Baltimore turnover of the game.

Morrall attempted a play that recalled the loss to the Jets, the flea flicker. He tried to lateral to Havrilak, but Havrilak couldn't see Morrall, because Jethro Pugh had blocked his sight, so Earl threw a pass for John Mackey, who was open. Before the ball reached Mackey, however, Eddie Hinton stepped in front and caught it. He headed for the end zone, where he was hit at the one, and fumbled. Seven players from both teams tried unsuccessfully to pick up the ball but couldn't. It finally was called a touchback when the ball rolled out of the end zone.

The Cowboys, jealous of all the Colts' turnovers, performed one of their own. Morton was intercepted by Rick Volk when Jim Duncan tipped the pass, and Volk returned the ball to the Dallas three-yard line. Tom Nowatzke scored for Baltimore, and O'Brien executed his first successful kick of the day. Score tied, 13–13.

Colt linebacker Mike Curtis intercepted with less than a minute to go. After two plays the young man the Colts nicknamed Lassie, for his long hair, was called in. He had missed two kicks that day, and there were only nine seconds left to play. Curry snapped, Morrall spotted, and O'Brien put his foot into the ball. When the scoreboard clock ticked off the final seconds, the score read BALTIMORE 16, DALLAS 13. A drained Bubba Smith watched Lassie's kick sail straight and stay straight, inside the right goal post by seven feet. He looked to his left and saw Bob Lilly, a Dallas defensive tackle, take off his helmet and throw it forty feet into the air. It was the best Dallas throw of the game, and number 78 whispered, "We did it."

Sandusky put his arm around Bubba's shoulder and smiled. They walked toward the locker room as pandemonium engulfed the Orange Bowl. A body flew out of the stands, and reflexively Bubba caught it before it hit the ground. "Sandusky began beating the person," Bubba remembers. "I looked down and realized it was Stanley "Crocked" Cohen. The Counselor was so happy for me, he had almost committed suicide. I yelled, "No, John, it's my pardner!" He gave the liquor-plastered Stanley to his friends, who were still horrified by his sudden leap."

In the locker room he sat on his stool waiting for the thrill of victory to engulf him, or whatever was supposed to happen. He waited; nothing happened. "I didn't feel any different. I began to feel disappointed over my lack of feeling—here I was, All-Pro for the second straight year, a member of a Super Bowl–winning team, without a broken bone in my body; and fifteen thousand dollars richer, and nothing felt unusual," recollects Bubba. He stood under the shower for fifteen minutes, letting the water flow over his numb body; dried off; smoked three Winstons; dressed, refused interviews, and climbed onto the team bus; stayed at the hotel long enough to call his happy parents; and left.

He walked alone toward the Miami beach. There would be no team party this year: no drinking; merely peace. Joy screamed from celebrations along and around the beach. He walked, without swagger, in the warm night air, looking up into the purple-black sky, which blinded white stars. He saw one, to his right . . . toward the north. It was the brightest, and he smiled, finally.

Twelve hours later he was back in the cold, back with the best fans in the East, the proud Baltimore crazies who knew their sports—the parade, the hoopla, the confetti, applause, horns, handshakes, and adulation for their heroes. Stanley was there—he remained blasted for a week. Bubba had discovered a new lady, a Washington model, whose high-cheeked copper beauty adorned every black magazine cover in the nation. He had caught the fever, and his happy thermometer had gone over the top and exploded with pride.

The rings for the champions had been presented. His name and position, the year, and team name were engraved around a huge diamond. Along with the ring was a replica for the player's lady. In mock sadness his much-used engagement ring was introduced to her mama, for some fine mama in his future. Stanley, who knew its history, read a funeral for the ring. Like an aging cantor he tolled the many names of the many ladies who had worn it. Both Bubba and Stanley laughed throughout the ceremony.

From a diamond ring to a telephone ring—it was Tody, bearing news. He was chosen first pick by the Dallas Cowboys—1971 and the Smiths were cooking—although it had been a disappointing season for USC. One of the problems had been Tody's ankle, reinjured in the Nebraska game, just when he was beginning to get hot. Two weeks earlier, while the team got ready for their game with Alabama, the black players had begun to receive letters, and they weren't love notes from adoring fans. One read, "We're gonna hang yo' ass to a tree." Others had the same objective, to frighten, and they succeeded. Most of the young men had never been to Alabama, and all they knew was that the state had a long record of black misery and death. Some of the players purchased Saturday night specials. Tody had never allowed himself the luxury of fear; he followed the instructions of street people, "Get them before they get you." Smitty's and Georgia's firmness, though, checked him, and Tody tried to relax.

When the team arrived, a photograph of Tody on the front page of a leading Birmingham newspaper greeted them, and the caption quoted a soon-to-be-famous member of the Alabama team, John Hannah: "I want him." The fear departed and the anger took hold, and Smith, that hot Deep South night, "Almost killed Hannah."

Next it was John Rodgers and Nebraska, and number 93, Tody, made sixteen unassisted tackles before his celebrated ankle gave way, fractured. Rated second among college football players before the Nebraska game, the injury prevented him from playing the rest of the season.

Now it was Tody and Bubba, two professionals, talking with each other about money, contracts, and what their sport had turned into—a business—and Bubba about to reach his peak, and Tody ready to make the climb. Beaver, however, had to make a hard decision—it was time to call a halt to his football career and become a businessman. He had accomplished many feats on the field, and he had passed the torch to his grateful brothers.

Bubba began thinking about himself and his accomplishments, and he decided he was worth more than he was receiving. He was playing three positions and taking home only one salary. Carroll Rosenbloom, the sports businessman par excellence, received him the next day. The graciousness of the meeting evaporated as soon as the ugly word *renegotiation* was spoken. The gray-haired millionaire turned a shade paler and quickly said, "It's not Colt policy, Bub." Smith, having learned a few things from his earlier contract negotiations, began reading from a prepared list of his accomplishments since his arrival in Baltimore. Rosenbloom, sticking firmly to his golden guns, reiterated his earlier statement. "Policy my ass," roared Bubba. The two exchanged a few heated remarks, and Smith fell back to his second position. He demanded a token gesture: a house, a lavishly furnished dream house in the name of

Charles Aaron Smith. Rosenbloom refused, and Bubba left, but not before making an appointment with the secretary for round 2.

Driving away, he saw exactly what he had been talking about with Massa Rosenbloom. Carroll did have an air of being the master of his slaves, but Number 78 had been free a long time, so free that he would buy his big house now and make them pay for it later. It was six blocks from Pimlico race track, the home of champions, and he considered himself just that when he made the deal, with Stanley's legal aid, to purchase it.

Three months later 6212 Stratmore Street was the fashion ideal of modern Baltimore. A designer was engaged—"This faggot came up with some great ideas"—and the three bedrooms were transformed into two, and the master bedroom was elevated a foot. His directions to the designer were basic: "The place must be so laid that a lady would feel uncomfortable in her clothes!" And it was, a dream come true. The bedroom drapes were blended orange, purple, and red. The wall to wall carpeting, an inch and a half of deep raspberry, blended with chocolate-red walls. Behind the mammoth bed a floor-to-ceiling cheetah skin turned to become a humongous television screen. Mirrors were everywhere, the largest over the bed, and fountains spouted rainbows. A magnificent swimming pool built in a figure 8, the second number on his jersey, topped off what it was, without doubt, laid, Bubba, laid. A sports Busting palace it became, and most of the female pulchritude that flowed in and out, like the fountains, discovered what *goal posts* really meant. In the Smith garage stood two brand-new automobiles a Corvette for the ladies who qualified and a Cadillac for the massa of the big house.

The atmosphere of the house was so compelling that confirmed bachelor, running partner, counselor, and dwarf companion, Stanley Cohen, fell in love with a beautiful lady, runner-up in the Miss Universe contest, named Artis. They were married, and Bubba had a part-time partner.

Bubba soon discovered he had moved directly across the street from Mamala Cohen, and every Friday Stanley would appear and drag the otherwise occupied bachelor over to Mama Cohen's place. It seemed to Bubba that Israel had invaded Stratmore Street—grandparents by the hundreds, and grandchildren by the thousands, and folks with tiny little hats by the ton. He ate heartily before attending because he knew what faced him, the dreaded matzo and that funny fish. Love poured out, and he moved to reciprocate—he presented Stanley's father, Gee Cohen, with his Lineman of the Year award. "You don't vant it?" the senior Cohen asked. "I'll get another," replied Bubba.

The Colts' year was good but not good enough for Baltimore, for they demanded a winner and nothing less. The Miami Dolphins beat them for the American Football Conference title, 21–0. The only fun Bubba had that day was when he chased Mercury Morris toward the Dolphin bench and Donald Shula. Number 78 wound up to hit them both, if he could control his aim, but Merc ducked, and Shula was flattened. A few of the word combinations coach Shula chose after the incident impressed even the rawest of the players.

Bub won All-Pro and Lineman of the Year again, yet the team had lost, and he promised himself an even better year to come.

The loss to Miami prevented another dream from coming true. Bubba, since learning of his brother's new job, had hoped all season to play against the Cowboys, the year of Cowboy Tody. It was perfect—the young man who had posed for publicity pictures in western garb, reminiscent of the movie *The Wild Bunch* was a perfect American Cowboy hero.

Freeze, Tody's best friend, asked to give an analysis of him, said "One quarter of his life is spent on the toilet; one quarter on the phone; the other half is a true friend and a hell of an athlete." To others he was Bubba's little brother, and they expected the same. Another group saw the celebration of color and style in his dress and heard his highly opinionated views and, perhaps frightened, branded him a militant, conceited peacock. The facts: he was among the most sought-after collegiate athletes in the country and completely secure in his being an intelligent black American.

Tom Landry, the coach of the Dallas Cowboys, symbolizes the computer age. Apparently he has little or no sense of humor and never trusts anyone—even his talented quarterbacks have been puppets on his string. Every play is called from the sidelines, and the nickname given him by Duane Thomas, the Plastic Man, seems perfect. Landry, a master technician, studied under the god of coaching, Vince Lombardi. Tody, the master of himself, had proven his value as a player under two of the great coaches in the history of the game, his father and John McKay.

There was no way in this world that these two men could have understood each other. Add race, and it proved to be another example of the widening gap between middle-aged white coaches and young black athletes. They marched to the beat of different distant drummers. It was James Brown singing with Lawrence Welk.

Duane Thomas, who preceded Tody's arrival by one year, had already caused a commotion within the superstructure of the Cowboys, finally refusing to speak to anyone; then Tody held out, finally coming to terms during Dallas's first exhibition game.

At last here came the forever-talking and magnetic El Toro, driving into Dallas, Texas, in the finest car imaginable, with the loudest tapes imaginable, and ready to take up where he had left off with the Wild Bunch. The only bunch in the Cowboys had been trained to be boy scouts. And turned their heads away upon Tody's arrival and sucked their tongues, *tsk, tsk,* what have we got here? The bonus baby from Hollywood?

Tody, always brilliantly alive, had gone to a university four miles from the land of fantasy, and he payed the price. Add technicolor costumes, addiction for the rookie, and there was no way he could avoid problems.

Trouble first arose three miles from the stadium. He saw an apartment he wanted and had placed a crisp one-hundred-dollar bill down as a deposit. When he returned to move in, a woman, vaguely reminiscent of the wicked witch in *The Wizard of Oz,* came to the door. Her husband, armed with a rifle, stood a dozen yards behind her. "We don't want yo' money, nigger." Most people frown at least when called that: Tody smiled; his body, and fist, frowned. He snatched the bill, which was in her burning hand, and spit through his Smith gap right in her muddy left eye. He booked and waited for the shot. None came, and so he drove away to find an even better pad on the fashionable North Side.

The shot came the next day in practice. Everyone knew him from the newspaper stories, and the witch informed the Cowboys about his "disgusting behavior." The Dallas front office called, and his punishment for behavior unworthy of the Cowboy image was assignment to the taxi squad, the squad of players who do not perform, only practice. Hitting the sled, a heavy machine built to resemble a padded lineman. "Fifty times, Smith." He obeyed, believing it was the Cowboy style. He was firing up to hit it the forty-sixth time and trembling with exhaustion when coach Landry iced by. "Not in shape for major league football, Smith?" Drained after completing his fifty, he sat down on the bench and, amazed, watched his teammates hit and drive the sled three times each. Tody, like Bubba, remembered his father's words, *be twice as good.* "Never be a quitter," his mother had said, and the words and the young man's belief in his talent helped him push his body into remarkable shape.

The team started out the season poorly. Landry was using two quarterbacks, Craig Morton, the incumbent, and Roger Staubach, the aspirant, and he was calling the plays for both from the sidelines. After losing three of his first seven games, Landry made a decision. He gave the quarterbacking job to Staubach on a regular basis but continued to insist upon calling the play for him. The result—nine straight victories. (Number 85 was used sparingly his rookie year, but when he played, he played well, and the fans loved his excitement.)

It was another Smith Super Bowl in 1972, this time presented in Tulane Stadium, New Orleans, Louisiana. Tody had made two friends on the team, Herb Adderly and, surprisingly, Roger Staubach. Despite Staubach's All-American, clean-cut look, he was found to be a man, a man of compassion, and he didn't pretend to be a god like some of the other players. Nor did he have any so-called race problems with other players. "He was a pure leader," says Tody, "a straight-out hope-to-die adult." The team, however, contained personality conflicts, problems that lasted into the preparations for the Super Bowl. Two days before the game of games a fight between two of the team's better athletes began on New Orleans' Bourbon Street and ended the next day on the practice field. Disorder was so rife, coach Landry called a team meeting and threatened everyone with fines, yet the Cowboys were six point favorites to win.

On the eve of the Super Bowl, Joe Frazier, the heavyweight champion, and Terry Daniels, a twenty-five-year old former SMU football player who aspired to own the New York Giants, were paired in the first heavyweight title bout held in New Orleans since 1892. Frazier knocked Daniels out in the fourth round. Daniels had absorbed an extraordinary beating, and he left the ring under his own power, his face a mixture of blood and welts. He was crying. Somebody said, "Let's hope the Dolphins put up a better fight tomorrow."

An addled nursery rhyme, which plagued the Cowboy franchise for years, was recalled the morning of the game after the team had been waiting twenty minutes for their buses: Monday's child is full of grace; Tuesday's child is fair of face; Wednesday's child has far to go; and—hold it, baby, 'cause the Dallas Cowboys have been trying to get past Wednesday for so long, there have been years when it looked as though they were telling time with a calendar instead of a wristwatch. And an advertisement in the New Orleans *Times-Picayune* read SWAP: TWO SUPER BOWL TICKETS FOR A .38 OR .45 AUTOMATIC. But the Cowboys won, 24–3.

Tody Smith collected his money and told Tango, "I never want to be here in this Cowboy uniform again. I'll never wear my championship ring." She understood—she had been with him through his pain. His team had won the championship of professional football, but Tody saw that most of them were amateurs in life. However much Tody wanted to leave the Cowboys, though, he had a contract, and if he didn't play for the champs, he wouldn't play at all. (The spring brought Tody a new problem. Playing a pickup basketball game with Jim Brown, the greatest rusher in National Football League history, and Tim Brown, another brilliant professional, Tody tore a cartilage in his right knee.

Bubba ended a four-day holdout and, disgruntled, traveled to Tampa, Florida, to begin the final year of his contract. Angry at the new general manager, Joe Thomas, Bubba wanted to leave the Colts and join perhaps his ex–check payer, Carroll Rosenbloom. Rosenbloom had magically made a deal that rocked football. He had originally purchased the Baltimore team for fifty thousand dollars; now the franchise was worth in excess of forty million, but he owed enormous taxes. The solution: he swapped franchises with Robert Irsay, who had made his bundle in air conditioners and owned the Los Angeles Rams. The exchange rendered Rosenbloom's taxes null and void. Carroll had escaped in great financial condition and had avoided fulfilling a promise made to Bubba to set him up in business. Bubba had gotten his house in the end, but Rosenbloom had not lived up to the real deal.

He reported for the game, and an upright pole held in the frozen-minded hands of Robert Lastra destroyed his right knee. The year of the Watergate burglary meant more pain for Charles Aaron Smith than for Nixon.

Bubba Smith, his huge, muscled body prone on a mobile

stretcher, stared at the ceiling. Snow white-uniformed creatures looked down at him. He had spent twenty-seven years getting used to people looking up at him; now he felt small, helpless. The doctor said, "It'll take an hour," and the anesthesiologist gave him the preparatory shot for the operation. Like any other patient asked to count backwards from one hundred, he began; unlike most he finished his one hundred and waited for another command. The anesthesiologist looked perplexed. Had he filled the hypodermic with the right amount? He hadn't realized, however, who he was dealing with—this was no average dude, this was a champion. He asked Bubba to count again, and after ninety-nine, the man gently guided Bubba into a world of dreams. A chase—everyone raced after him, and refused to be captured. He awoke hours later, kicking and moaning. A nurse who accidentally stepped into the path of his kick understood how an athlete felt playing against the patient when she came to.

He came out from under the drugs and, remembering, thought Am I gonna play again? His doctor hovered over him. A nurse asked, "How did it go, Doc?" He answered, "Fine, but it'll take a lot of work." Bubba knew the work—he had watched his brother Beaver recuperate—but he questioned the word *fine*. The doctor had anticipated an hour, and Bubba, from the wall clock, calculated six. Six damn hours—what did he do to me? He was wheeled out—bottles clanged against the metal rods that rolled with him—and he heard someone say, "That's Bubba Smith, poor thing." That August morning he returned to a dream world mouthing the words *poor thing*.

Hours after the surgery, after the visitors had left, the pain rushed back like a thunderbolt, "like a million toothaches in your knee!" he says. He smashed the call button, which alerted the Nightingale, and she quickly responded. She injected morphine, and he awaited the results. "Every four hours I'll return with some help," she cheerfully said, waving the syringe. It sounded reasonable. He adjusted his back and lay there for hours investigating his body. Nervously he pushed his hand, the wrist taped, through his hair, as if the gesture would help the knifing pain vanish. The *needle* came minutes later. The medical term is *tempered;* liquor drinkers call it cutting; and the injured hate the sound of either word—the following doses of morphine were less potent than the first to avoid causing addiction to the powerful drug. The cracking ache stayed with him, slowed now and then every four hours but was always there.

The pain was controlled with Percodan, and it helped for a moment. Bubba forced himself to wait for the prescribed time, but World War VI was rehearsing in his leg, and he couldn't take it anymore. He called, waited, called three times; there was no response. At last she came, a bruiser he hadn't seen before, and he was yelling at her. She threw the Percodan at him. "You're an athlete, catch," she said. He did, and she stood there gloating. He grabbed his bedpan, and in a blinding motion threw it at her, screaming, "Catch this, bitch!"

The white-clad therapist even appeared bored with herself. "Go to the rail. Learn how to walk," she ordered.

The sweat popped like fat from a frying pan. He forced himself out of the wheelchair for the first time. He was weak from lying in bed these weeks, and his body trembled. Two steps, and a fog rose in his body. He struggled against passing out and strove to place himself back in the chair. The therapist calmly walked over to him and slid him against the wall. He had made it two steps, and instead of applause he had received a frown.

Crossing the room, she passed by him—twenty feet of vacant room but she chose to pass close to him, hitting his cast. The chair turned over with a slam. He didn't attempt to right himself. Like a huge snail he inched his way toward her. Somehow he lifted a two-and-a-half weight that was lying unused on the floor and crept closer. When he thought he was near enough, he raised the iron and belted her in the back of her tousled head.

He was released three days later to mend in his castle. Stanley and his wife moved in and cooked and cleaned for him. The pain lingered, but at least he was surrounded by people he loved.

Having worn the cast for seven weeks, he was at his doctor's office. An athlete without the use of his limbs is like a pianist without fingers or a painter without sight, and he tensely watched the cast removed. His leg, formerly bowed, was now straight for the first time in his life, but his knee resembled a balloon, and he screamed when he saw the leg above the knee—it looked one hundred years old. The muscles had atrophied, and the skin hung down like spaghetti. It would take months to build up, he thought, months, if ever.

His doctor, recognizing Bubba's fear, sent him to Children's Hospital, and the magic worked for him. When he wheeled into the hospital, he saw them, hundreds of tots, infants, innocent kids, many of them in casts, some in body casts, dozens in traction, and it was wheelchair city. They looked at him and seemed to wonder why the big fellow looked so sad. He looked at them, and they were laughing, giggling, and making the best of it. "Here I was," he recalls, "having lived twenty-seven years with extremely good fortune, and there they were, two- and three-year-old children fighting back. They weren't letting it beat them, and I was."

It had run its course, the right-knee, from Doll to Beaver to Tody and now Bubba. Smitty had discovered that he could guide talent with one leg, but his sons were both one hundred pounds or more heavier, and they were players.

Bubba found himself in the Colt locker room during one of the team's weekday practices. He missed the men and needed the atmosphere. In the middle of a conversation with Johnny Unitas about the Colts' poor season, J. U. was asked to take a phone call. Bubba waited patiently, talking with a few of the veterans. Unitas returned and apologized for the long wait. The call he had received was from general manager Joe Thomas, who had informed him, by telephone, that he was benched for the remainder of the season.

The modern maximum quarterback, John Unitas, unutterably square—who had come into football on the end of a sixty-cent phone call, a call asking him if he was still looking for work; who in 1958, fourteen years before the latest phone call, had brought the Baltimore Colts their first championship in the first pro football game ever to be played with a sudden-death fifth quarter; who, a mature, modest, nonswinging professional, had always listened respectfully to his coaches—had been handed his walking papers by telephone.

If a white man who brought his team from a fifty-thousand-dollar risk by Carroll Rosenbloom to a forty-million-dollar franchise can be treated like that, what chance have I got? thought a shocked Bubba. That means Bub don't mean shit to them! The news chased Bubba back to his daily workouts.

Tody limped into the 1972 season.

He played superbly. He was on the first team and played as his father had taught him to. Number 85 was on his game, sacking everybody, until halfway into the season he began to feel strange, couldn't sleep, often vomited, and felt oddly tired. He began taking Bennies to give himself some pep, but nothing seemed to help him lose his extraordinary fatigue. Sometimes he had a difficult time walking off the field after the pills had worn off. The Cowboys' doctor prescribed "some wine—you're uptight."

During a game against the San Francisco 49ers, he knew something was seriously wrong. He had shied away from three tackles, and John Brody, the 49er quarterback, looked as if he were moving in slow motion. He left the team and flew to Los Angeles. The thought that he might be losing control of himself was flashed through his mind, and he went to see a psychiatrist. When Tody walked in, he was willing to do anything he was told, but a half hour later the doctor said to him, "You need a woman to make you feel successful." A huge medical dictionary came flying through the air at the psychiatrist's head. "The only reason I missed killing him was because I was sick," says Tody. Of all prescriptions to give a lady's man and a successful professional athlete!

He finally got the word—he had mononucleosis—but only after his parents took matters in hand. His father had routinely called him to say they would see him at Thanksgiving. Tody replied, "I'll see you if I'm alive." Smitty and Georgia were at his house in four hours. Smitty went to the Cowboy front office and demanded that his son be hospitalized. Tests revealed the severity of Tody's illness, and he was ordered to stay in bed. If he had played another game, his spleen would have ruptured, and he would have died.

Despite his condition the team wanted him to play two weeks later. Tody asked for the opinion of a second doctor. He begged for assistance from the Cowboy front office, and two days later he was headed toward Rochester, Minnesota, to the Mayo Clinic.

When Tody arrived in the Gopher State he felt like anyone but Paul Bunyan—he had lost thirty pounds during the season. He almost crawled from the taxi to the hospital entrance. "Snow was everywhere, and it helped me to know that if I fell, I wouldn't hurt myself," he remembers.

"They seemed to know I was coming. Two attendants rushed to help me as I glided through the revolving door. 'Right this way Mr. Smith,' they said, 'We have your room ready.'" He was guided to his floor. An ever-smiling male nurse opened a huge door. "I heard it, the click, when the doors closed behind them—the sound of a lock shutting. I thought it unusual, but it was Mayo—who knew what was supposed to happen?"

The nurse ushered him into his room, and he noticed a

second unusual feature of the hospital. "There were no ornaments, no pictures, no telephone, no television, nothing." And the walls were rubbery.

What was there was a bed, and that was what he needed most of all, a bed and a good smoke. He reached into his inside jacket pocket bringing forth a new pack of cigarettes, and placed a cigarette in his mouth as though it were a tiny bar. He sat back on the bed and lit it. The first exhalation of smoke had not reached its limit before a nurse rushed in, saying "No smoking, Mr. Smith." She stood there before him, a well-mannered smile dimpling her cheeks—stood long enough to take his pack of cigarettes, as well as the one he had lit. She had what she wanted, and she left.

His first visitor was a blonde young woman. A plain-looking farm girl sort. She entered without knocking, and Tody was in the middle of undressing. Only his shoes, socks, and underwear stood in the way of his being naked. The woman shrieked, "You have my pants on!" She repeated the accusation three times. Tody, trying his damndest not to laugh—he thought he had forgotten how—pushed the call button. A blinding moment later the nurse came. She ordered the woman out of the room and apologized to Tody. "White folks have always been wierd to me," he says, "but this girl had me looking to see if I had her pants on for a minute."

His aloneness didn't last long. He had stretched out on the bed, and was wearing the hospital smock and considering his first visitor. He awaited the doctor, but what he received was a thirty-year-old chubby, prickish man. He entered and sat on Tody's bed, and Tody frowned, his tongue searching every inch of his mouth.

At last the man lifted his head and twinkled his blue eyes—he resembled a cartoon cupid adorning an unimaginative Valentine's Day card.

"How many?" he asked.

Smith cocked his head. "Wot?"

"How many times?"

"Do I know you?" asked Tody.

"How many times did you do it?"

"It—what is IT?" pleaded Tody.

"HOW MANY TIMES DID YOU DO IT!" he screamed.

"DO WHAT, MOTHER FUCKER?"

The man rolled up the sleeves of his bathrobe and exposed seventeen scars on his wrists—razor cuts.

"HOLY SHIT!" cried Tody, and the button was pushed. The

nurse came again and commanded the man out of the room. She was about to leave when Tody, who hadn't made up his mind whether to laugh or cry, said to her, "Er, miss . . . hey, miss is this . . . er, floor . . . for the . . . " He trailed off, and the nurse completed the question for him. "The emotionally disturbed?"

"Is that anything like a nut house?" She shook yes and booked.

So did Tody, down the hall to the pay phone, where other odd creatures winked, blinked, nodded, and whatever else. Dialing furiously, he was calling coach Landry. But he wasn't home. He tried three other numbers; no one answered.

As Tody dragged his body back to his room, a commotion began at the far end of the hallway, and he froze. An elderly hunchbacked man had swallowed something the wrong way, and five of his fellow patients were beating his hunchback with their fists. On first glance they appeared to be helping him to cough up the problem, yet he was bleeding and bellowing in pain from the blows, which could be heard throughout the ward. A battalion of attendants saved him from destruction and his would-be murderers returned placidly to their dinners.

Tody reversed himself and sped back to the telephone, and he reached Landry. "I warned him that if I stayed another hour in this crazy house, I would kill everyone in the ward and then tell the world that he drove me to it!" He hung up the phone so hard that the cradle cracked in half. Exhausted, he walked back to his room and laid his body on the bed. In walked seven doctors, six white, one Asian, all with pads and pencils ready for note taking. Tody looked at each. They all seemed quite serious and eager to help. "I thought to myself, If I know Landry, I'll be out of here in an hour. Let's have some fun at their expense."

They asked what all psychiatrists ask. He was stone silent. Twenty questions and ten minutes passed, and after every question, which he refused to answer, his eyes met the Asian doctor's. He was the only one who didn't look crazy. Finally he was fed up with the bullshit. He took the middle finger of both hands, stretched the ends of his mouth open, fluttered his tongue, wiggled his eyes. The doctor's pencils scribbled furiously, and when Tody thought they had covered that reaction, he pulled off the covers, reached for his penis, and began wagging it at them. They booked, and the Asian doctor winked as he left.

Something in Tody's manner over the phone must have impressed Landry. Forty-five minutes after the call, three gracious attendants, choked with apology, moved him to a medical ward. His treatment for mononucleosis began.

In Maryland another bed-ridden athlete could only dream of his cherished sport and recall the glory. Once, when the fairyland house was empty except for its master, two acquaintances came by to swap stories and keep Bubba company. Due to his size Bubba absorbed pain killers as if they were aspirin, and he needed a refill. One of the men, who was quite wealthy, introduced him to Quaaludes. The pain had been building in his leg, but after he took the pill, the pain disappeared and he felt like laughing at everything. The lude inspired him to grab his crutches and attempt to walk to the bathroom. His friends' cheers were the last thing he heard before he awoke minutes later, yet he felt euphoric. The man with the ludes had more. "Twenty thousand are buried in my back yard to keep them fresh. I'd be proud to give you some," he said, and Bubba accepted quickly. He needed something, he thought.

A guest Bubba did not need, a young man Bubba had spent time with, teaching him what he knew, came to visit. A talented youngster, he had graduated from Grambling and showed promise. He was at Bubba's bedside, looking at his teacher, and he said, "Well, I guess I'm the big man in town now." His words cut, yet Bubba responded, "Someone has to hold up the line." When the young man left, Bubba cried for his ungrateful pupil, alone.

"I thought everyone had left me," he says, and he decided to chance a visit to the outside world. He loaded himself up with his newly discovered miracle drug and went to a game at Memorial Stadium. He was in his wheelchair, and when he was introduced to his fans, they stood and screamed and applauded their fallen hero. Five minutes it took, and the tears fell again. Lydell Mitchell, a brilliant newcomer, had pushed him onto the field and afterwards helped him to a corner of the stadium.

He watched his friend Joe Willie Namath and the Jets tear the Colts apart the first half. His former student, who thought he was the big man now, was lost playing opposite Winston Hill. "Hill is the greatest holder to ever play the game of football," says Bubba, "a remarkably cunning athlete." Bubba asked an attendant to wheel him to the team bench; despite the young man's attitude, he was still a Colt. The new general manager, Joe Thomas, saw the wheelchair carrying the crippled player to the bench, and so had the fans, who were cheering him again, cheering him as if he could get up and stop the Jets' drive. Thomas yelled through the walkie-talkie the attendant bore, "Get him the fuck off the field." Both the attendant and Bubba ignored the scream. He was with his teammates now, and he waved for the young man to come over. "Move a little wider," he said. "Winston will have to reach for you, and the referee may see him holding you." The next time the defense took the field, the young man obeyed his teacher, and it worked. Many of the fans understood what had happened, and applauded Bubba a third time.

Bubba wanted his team to win—he always had been a freak for victory, and even in a wheelchair he couldn't shake the desire. The Jets destroyed the Colts that day, though, and when the game was over the teams left the field in a hurry, leaving Bubba alone behind the Colt bench. His leg hurt, and he wanted to get out of the stadium. The only player left was Joe Willie Namath, who saw him stranded, came across the field, and helped him off. "I know the feeling, Bub," he said. "Joe was a pure brother," Bubba says. Namath had thrown for five hundred yards that day, but he had time for a friend.

Brothers were exactly what Bubba needed, and a bond as strong as blood was strengthened by a common struggle. Tody was in Los Angeles, as was Beaver—where else should Bubba be? Stanley was his partner forever, but he was busy, being a new father. And Bubba had to get busy, rebuilding his body. In eight months he would have to perform again.

The Smiths hid themselves in Marina del Rey, and when they weren't exercising on the machines, working on their torn muscles, they soaked in steaming jacuzzis. A thousand reps a day on the leg machine for Bubba. Five miles a day of beach running for Tody. Work, hard and exhausting, but the only way to return to the game. The 'ludes and marijuana snapped them out of their nightmares but only for a moment.

A two-bedroom apartment occupied by Bubba and Tody and Tate, with friends and acquaintances, became poker headquarters. Freeze, Al Cowlings, O. J. Simpson, Isaac Curtis, Rudy Benjamin, Billy Parks, Curly Culp, Ahmad Rashad, Sidney Wickes, Curtis Rowe, Bernie Copeland, Miller and Mel Farr—on and on the roster went. They shared the great times and the problems, and they shared themselves and gave each other hope. All of them understood, because they were from the same world of fame and pain.

Bubba had forgotten romance; his companions were pain and escape. The knee refused to respond—it wouldn't bend. Dr. Robert Rosenfeld, a specialist many athletes respected, put Bubba to sleep and tried to bend it, with little success, though he suggested a program for recovery, and the daily workouts consumed Bubba.

By June he still couldn't run. Another doctor introduced him to black beauties. Now, he was a limping drug store, beauties to speed him up, and 'ludes to ease him down.

July 10, and he reported to camp. Two hundred eighty pounds of fear crammed with pills to help his body do what it used to do. He would do anything asked of him.

A new coach, a man who had worked under Don Shula, had replaced his friend McCafferty. When he arrived in his room, the phone was ringing, and the new coach greeted him, then surprised him with an order to be in full uniform in half an hour. "We're gonna have a live pass rush scrimmage," he said and wished him well. Bubba was worried. What is happening? he thought. On the very first day, in my condition, a scrimmage? I might get hurt. There are hungry rookies out there who need to feed their families and don't care about anyone else. I don't mind working with the veterans, but . . . He popped a beauty in his mouth and slowly left his room. As he walked to the field, he thought about the order and felt sure that the franchise couldn't mean to hurt him. He was a Colt, a hope-to-die Baltimore Colt, and he would be one until he retired. He stood with his teammates, everyone happy to see him, greeting him with friendly pats, slaps, and fives.

The names of the scrimmaging squads were called, and when the assistant said his name, he almost shit on himself. A whistle blew, and he snapped on his helmet and walked to the line. The feeling of being back almost overcame his fear. The black beauty had kicked in, and he went down to his stance. The ball was hiked, and for some reason the player who had lined up opposite him overplayed him, and Bubba sailed through an opening as wide as a Mack truck and touched the quarterback. Another whistle, and the coach took Bubba out with a nice-going slap on the butt. What is going on? he thought. He watched the team work six more plays, and then as suddenly as it had begun, it was over.

He hadn't broken a sweat, and he stayed as the others filed off. He was up now and wanted to experiment. Padded dummies were nearby in a cart, and he removed six, placed them on the field, and began an independent workout. He walked over to begin his run, and a coach ran onto the field and screamed at the top of his lungs, "No, no, no!"—a frantic cry. Bubba turned to ask him, "What's your problem?" The coach mumbled, "I'd rather you didn't do that now, Bub." "I know what I got to do," he said, but the coach was firm and left.

He still couldn't understand what was happening. Shaking his head, he strolled off, and two men, men he had never seen before, stood at the gate. One asked for his autograph, the other remarked on how good Bubba looked, and they left.

He couldn't eat lunch, and he couldn't sleep. He sat in his room. The phone rang. The afternoon practice would begin with group drills—would he teach the rookies, the young draft choices, how he sacked the quarterback? "Sure," he answered, and he began to feel needed again. He took a beauty and jogged out to reveal to each young man his trade secrets. Practice ended at 4:00.

He went back to his room, left to eat dinner and attend the team meeting, and by 8:30 returned to his room. A Quaalude was needed now to come down from his high, and he began to relax. His solitude was interrupted by a knock, the new head coach. "Joe Thomas would like to see you, Bub," he said. "There was that look of regret in his eyes," Bubba remembers, "and my mind began to race. 'You shitting me?' I asked." "Bring the play book," the coach said, and Bubba's heart stopped. Bring the play book—the death knell for a football player. He picked up the book and glanced at his jacket, and it read PROPERTY OF THE BALTIMORE COLTS, and he was just that. For five years he had thought, walked, breathed, and slept the Colts, and now he wasn't needed.

The coach's slick black hair was mussed on the sides of his head. Perhaps he had been running his hands through it. He looked hurt. It may have been an act, but he played it well, and Bubba followed him to the general manager's office. A thousand and one thoughts snaked through his mind. Who wants a cripple? he thought. I don't want to leave!

They were there, they had reached the office, and the door was open for him. They entered, and behind a desk a mile long sat Massa Thomas, arrogantly sneering at his slave, his property. "You've always talked about California, Smith—you're now an Oakland Raider!" A sick smile curled his no-lipped mouth, and the stink of his attitude led Bubba to move a step closer to him. One of his horses had broken its leg, Bubba said to himself, and now. . . . Like a quarterback he rifled the play book straight at Joe Thomas's head.

CHAPTER 8

Revelations

A BLACK PATCH COVERS the eye of the team emblem. A pirate—a fitting symbol for the then Oakland Raiders. But why would any professional football team, including a team of renegades, accept a near cripple in exchange for a healthy All-Pro tight end, Raymond Chester. Odder still, two years later, Bubba Smith, who could perform at a fraction of his former ability, saw his salary tripled. Was his lawsuit against the National Football League the motivation for unwarranted generosity of team to team (the trade between Baltimore and Oakland) and team to player (his raise later). The athlete was puzzled.

(The shock of his trade and the suspicion of deeper meaning intensified when the two men who had been just fans at the first-day tryouts in Baltimore turned up in Oakland as team scouts. During that morning scrimmage and afternoon lecture, he had already been the property of the Raiders. The workout was merely a modeling job for his new master, Al Davis.)

Hope, though, was in his heart, and it curtailed his curiosity. Even his brother Tody, who had had surgery, was certain of Bubba's return to form.

The years at Oakland faintly echoed his once thundering brillance, and he choked the muffled sounds with drugs. Quaaludes, black beauties, and codeine were ingested daily to kill any pain, much of it physical, but a lot of it caused by a cracked ego. A Smith from Boomahnt, however, can't live without laughter and love, and it came, in nature's way, on the first day he arrived in Oakland.

Bubba had called a friend to meet him at the airport. His friend, due to a work conflict, sent her two nieces, Wanda and Deborah—and Deborah and Deborah and Deborah. Green as the budding leaves of a young tree were her eyes, and the trunk and limbs were perfect. Bubba's thoughts branched out from his pain as she drove him to his training camp in Santa Rosa.

Waiting for his physical, he looked out the hotel window and found her with his eyes. She was gaily swinging on the park swings, and from a hundred yards he could feel her energy. Before practice, he stopped her swinging, and they made arrangements for the future.

He joined his teammates, pure, raw men—no poets were allowed on the Raiders—including the Soul Patrol: Willie Brown, George "Ack" Atkinson, Jack "Killer" Tatum, and Skip "Doctor Death" Thomas, all solid niggahs who loved living and took no mess.

During the season Bubba worked ten minutes a game and alternated with Tony Klein. Taped like a mummy, Bubba was entombed within drugs. The only ray of light came from Deborah Sam, his new lady.

(Tody, now a member of the Houston Oilers, was at his happiest since becoming a professional. His health was returning slowly, and he trusted and respected his coach, Sid Gilman. One of his all-time favorite straight-shooting friends, Billy Parks, was with him. He was making good money, and he was in love with his Tango. To top it all off, he was forty-five minutes from Beaumont.)

Bubba was clinging to life through Deborah, although he didn't know it himself. She was beautiful, but more important she was his friend. Under her parents' strict orders she couldn't move in with him, and he had to work at their relationship.

He kept in touch with his mother and father, though not as much as he had in his glory years. He had lost his pride.

His lack of self-esteem helped bring on pneumonia, and without his friend, Curly Culp, who carried Bubba on his back to the hospital one night in the summer of 1974, it may have been worse. Curly, a six-footer, two hundred eighty pounds of solid muscle, had been his friend since his first Pro Bowl, and proved it time and again.

People like Curly and Deborah may have "saved me from hurting myself," Bubba says. He knew that she was what he wanted, but he was so unsure of himself now that he distrusted his love for her. One Bay evening he proposed to her, and she booked, beat a path home and was back to his building in two hours with everything in her car. And would he, her intended, help her bring them in? "I've changed my mind," Bubba said, and poof, she vanished, and there was nothing but the sound of silence—and Bubba swallowing another Quaalude.

Two weeks later, or fourteen days, or a half a month, or three hundred thirty-six hours—it depends on how you count it; it felt more like a year to Bubba—she hadn't called. "I figured she would," Bubba remembers. "She never did. I dated a couple of ladies—they were boring. Deborah was the real deal." A shaken thirty-year-old athlete, eight years a professional, now severely injured and thoroughly confused, walked to his phone, picked up the receiver, dialed, and hung up. "I didn't know what to say! I took a Quaalude so if she told me to go to hell, I could stay mellow." He waited until the drug kicked in and slowly pushed numbers on the phone. Clearing his throat, adjusting his glasses, and relaxing against the couch, he was ready. After two rings she answered, and he said as quickly as possible, "This is Bubba. Sorry, I didn't mean the shit."

"Excuse me?" she said, barely able to understand him.

It had been hard enough to say it once; now he had to repeat it. He slowed down and repeated each word as if typing each letter. The chill thawed, and in two hours they were sitting next to each other watching *The Towering Inferno*.

Oakland's coach, John Madden, led his team of renegades to a fine year. Their first play-off game, against Miami, set the stage for a new scene in brother Tody's life. At home, after having led Houston in sacks in 1974, Tody was caught in a crossfire of affection. Georgia and Tate were leaving for a San Francisco shopping spree and the Oakland game when his mother asked his girlfriend, "When are you two going to make this legal?"

"Whenever Tody is ready," answered Tate.

"Sweetheart, did you hear that?" asked Mama.

"Yes, Mother I heard Tate," said Tody.

"It's none of my business, but I do think that you two—"

Before Mama could finish her cupid caper, Tody walked out of the room searching protection from the exploding shell fire.

"Sweetheart, I'm trying to talk to you about your life," Mama said.

"I know, Mama," he said patiently, biting his tongue.

"I don't think we should rush Tody if he's not sure of his love for me," Tate said.

"Sweetheart, do you think that your mother would dare rush you into such a wonderful thing as marriage . . . if I didn't think you were ready?"

Tody had discovered that the front lawn needed watering. The last time Lawrence Edward Smith had done any gardening dated back a few decades, but he now pursued it with vigor.

The bags were packed with Georgia care and placed within the trunk of Tody's Eldorado. The battle plan had given them a half hour of loving attack time and they were finding range. The first bombardment had been a few degrees beyond Tody, but they had a fix on him now.

The lawn was becoming a lake, and the water pressure and his defenses gave out at the same moment.

"Okay," said Tody, "isn't it time for you to get to the airport?"

"Whatever you say, sweetheart," chirped Mama.

"He's right mother," said Tate, prancing dutifully to the car.

Tody sloshed to his stylish chariot, eased his frame in, and sped off with a squeal. By the time the skycaps had taken the luggage, Tate had accepted Tody's proposal. Somewhere between the Beaumont airport and Blossom Street, Tody bellowed, "Next week!"

Somewhere between Beaumont and San Francisco Georgia Smith discovered that the handsomely rugged "Dandy" Don Meredith was flying up on the same flight to report the Oakland-Miami game. Before they landed, Meredith had accepted the invitation to the wedding of Tate and Tody.

Tody was set for the game. His television set was angled so he could watch his brother's team beat Miami, 21–20. A Kenny Stabler pass to Clarence Davis decided the contest. Lying next to Tody was a lovely fox who knew how lucky she was—Tody had told her how lucky moments before the Davis reception—but before settling down to celebrate the Oakland victory, Dandy Don told the world Tody Smith's wedding plans.

It took the brilliant mind of young Smith to explain Mr. Meredith's bulletin. "Dandy Don is blasted! He's talking about

Bubba and made a mistake. Wouldn't I have told you myself, darlin'?" Tody had done it again.

One month later there was a knock at the door of suite 65. It was the evening before Tate's and Tody's nuptials. A tender voice was heard on the other side of the door. "Who is it?"

"Me," exclaimed Tody.

"I can't let you in tonight, Tody," said Tate. "It's the night before we get married."

"SO WHAT?" asked Tody.

The door next to Tate's room opened—it was her mother. She whispered to her future son-in-law rules of etiquette. Tody listened, his handsome face transformed by astonishment. He about-faced, hurriedly down to the gambling tables, lost four hundred dollars, returned to his room, fell asleep and had a nightmare.

The next day it was all the wedding march at Cupid's Chapel on the Vegas strip. Everyone was there, everyone except Tody. Tody was in the bathroom. His friend Freeze had predicted it. Tody's usually bronze complexion was snow white. In the past twelve hours the truth had hit him like a block of cement. He had awakened from his nightmare ringing wet, unable to sleep. Two hundred thirty pounds of muscle sat on the toilet, silk-striped tuxedo pants draped over his mirror-polished shoes, a dazed Adonis frozen in fear, praying that is was merely a fantasy. Good friend Freeze interrupted his trip and shook him into readiness.

The taped Cupid's Chapel Wedding March began, and Tody was shoved into position by Freeze and Bubba, the best man. Accompanying the melodious march was a live drum beat. Bubba and Freeze searched for the source of the thudding. Bubba, standing closest to Tody, discovered it, because Tody's tuxedo jacket rose and fell with every beat—it was from the groom's heart pumping. To top it off, in came the preacher, a five-foot-nine flaming queen whose eyelashes batted like moth's wings. Bubba, like Tody, was as loose as a goose, 'lude loaded back, and both had played sincerity to a bust, but when the gay minister looked at Tody as he read the oath to Tate and said, "Do you take this gorgeous hunk of man for your lawful husband," Bubba broke his cool and began his air-hammer laugh. Joy overcame the guests, and the ceremony, a Las Vegas miracle, concluded.

Standing near Smitty and Georgia was lovely Deborah Sam,

wondering what she was getting into. Mama's gaze locked on Bubba, a look that said, "You're next." As usual Mama was right. Five months later, four hundred guests from all over the country came to Las Vegas for the union. The MGM Grand Hotel's wedding present was two hundred rooms for Mr. Smith's and the future Mrs. Smith's guests.

On the day of the wedding Deborah knocked on the door to his suite. Bubba, blasted on 'ludes, opened the door and asked, "What time is it?" Was he late for the ceremony? "Bubba, we must get the license." "Go get it," he said.

Six hours later the last of the Smiths was hitched in front of a standing-room-only crowd smothered in mink, dripping diamonds, and loaded with ex-girlfriends. Although the casting call was answered by the same lightweight preacher, Bubba, benefitting from rehearsal, held onto his composure. Most of the Soul Patrol, though, fell out. After the ceremony Bubba yelled playfully at the rice throwers, "Would you cut that shit out? You're ruining my suit."

Get down! The downbeat was struck, and the dance floor filled. Get Down! The electric bass gave the heartbeat a body, and they danced. Get Down! Smokey Robinson's uniquely vulnerable sound guided the dancers, and the beautiful people worked on some moves. Get down they did, celebrating the Bubba-Deborah nuptials. It was like a miniature Mardi Gras, that night in Vegas—everyone who was anyone turned out and turned on, and by the time they had turned in, it was dawn and the Las Vegas odds makers would have placed bets that it had been the best get down witnessed in the famous open-all-night city. The odds makers would have ended their careers on poverty row, however, if they had gambled on the marriage between the superstar and his wondrously lovely lady lasting more than a month.

From the neon of Vegas to their penthouse in Oakland the newlyweds went. They had it all—the objects, the toys, the wardrobe, the cars, the money—everything any newly married modern American couple dreams of, except understanding. The champion Smith, the possessor of a new two-year-no-cut contract that paid him triple what he had made in his Baltimore glory years, was in love, no question, but he couldn't love in return. The back-at-cha was missing. His unarticulated fear of failure, his crushed pride, the deterioration of what, he thought, made him loved, prevented him from reaching out to Deborah. He was a spoiled, crippled brat who could relate only to the perfection of his sport. Darling Deborah, at that time a model BAP, a black American princess, hadn't been trained to be a supportive wife/woman; she was a girl in love with a hero.

Bubba needed a level head to control his emotions, but the Quaaludes, the cocaine, and black beauties took him on a roller coaster ride. When he came down it was to a reality that focused on his pain and the collapse of his career. He refused to deal—and went up again. He was bitter to those who had sent him on that ride. An experience that illuminated the newlyweds' apartness involved a puppy named Kiska, a bitch who adored her master. She was a gift from Tody, the owner of prize malumute dam Khiana.

One evening Kiska greeted Bubba, who had returned from practice tired and thoroughly disgusted with his lameness. He had hoped for a hot meal, like those Mama made, but twenty seconds into his castle princess Deborah asked to be taken out. Bub popped a Quaalude, picked up Kiska, went out onto the penthouse balcony, and climbed up to the roof, the dog in his arms. Six-foot-nine Bubba began discussing his problems in depth with Kiska. Malumutes are inclined to howling, and hearing her master's tale of woe, she sang her sad song. Consoled, he told her more. Deborah strode onto the balcony and began to complain, her green eyes shining brighter than usual as she tried to talk to her man. After every sentence both Bubba and Kiska bayed at the stars. Deborah booked, and Bubba and Kiska continued their duet.

Three weeks later the Smith's were divorced, and Bubba was gone from the Oakland Raiders. It was up to him—he had a no-cut contract—but he couldn't stay in the same city with the lady he truly loved, and couldn't live with.

The year 1975 was tough for Southwestern Bell, which lost thousands of dollars in unmade telephone calls from Tody to Bubba. "Every Sunday before we play, I spend a half hour to forty-five minutes on the phone with Bubba in Oakland going over the offensive tackle I'll be facing," declared Tody in an interview with Bob West of the Port Arthur, Texas, *News*. "Bubba being here is a lifelong dream come true. If I don't work harder and get better, Bubba will have my job. Don't let anybody kid you about him being over the hill."

The legend had returned to B. S. country. The dream fulfilled, echoed Smitty and Georgia from their home—two of their three young men near home. Bubba Smith was back where he grew up, down-home with the Houston Oilers, and the largest city in the South welcomed the largest pro football brothers in the country. Tody, playing his heart out and his ass off for the team, would have Bubba as his backup.

Bum Phillips, the new coach of the Oilers, had known Coach Smith for twenty years. Bum had started coaching in Nederland, Texas, and had moved to Beaumont's French High School. The two high school coaches had grown up in football together. "If Coach Smith was a white man, he would have had my job," said Phillips.

The future, but for the truth, couldn't have looked brighter. Smitty and Georgia had seen Bubba play in Oakland and had remarked on the difference in their son's ability, and Bubba had told Tody a few of the facts on the phone, but no one except the man himself knew the full extent of the problem. Not until Bubba moved in with Tody in Houston did Tody begin to understand the whole truth.

Tody thought Bubba's moodiness grew out of the divorce. He searched and uncovered his old black book, which contained the phone numbers and the ratings of every available fox in the country. No 10's for El Toro; his infamous catalogue began at 1,000,000. The cover of his research book was engraved T. S. COUNTRY AKA COCO-BRONZE HEAVEN. But Bubba's angels were in his pills. He'd lock himself in his room, and the only way Tody could break into his world, a wall away, was to telephone him.

If the Oilers record had been better, Tody probably would have been selected an All-Pro in 1975. Although the team featured Curly Culp, Billy "White Shoes" Johnson, and other fine talents, the Oilers failed to make the play-offs. Bubba started in only two games, both against former coaches. Bubba's insight, Phillips knew, into the game plan of Madden of Oakland and Shula of Miami could be decisive.

For the Miami game Bubba loaded up. He knew that his former coach would run directly at the Houston weakness. It was Shula's style, and Bubba was the weakness. He was higher than the top of the Astrodome before the opening kickoff. His teeth were chattering so loudly, he wondered if his mother and father, sitting in the stands, could hear them. Shula will try to show the world that I can't play anymore. He may be right, but I'm ready, Bubba thought.

The game proved Bubba right on time. Against a team that had won seven straight games, Bubba collected twelve unassisted tackles, two sacks of quarterback Bob Griese, a blocked extra point, and a blocked field goal attempt by Garo Yepremian. The champion had saved it for his final game. Houston won, 20–19. It was his swan song.

The year 1976 was a year of retirement. The greatest coach in high school football history, Willie Ray Smith, Sr., left his post after wrestling with the problems caused by the token racial integration of the 1960's. The black schools were raided by white high schools, and the talent left. What replaced successful athletics were youngsters confused by dope. Coach Smith had given his heart to young men for years, and he received public appreciation on May 28, 1976, when Beaumont, Texas, was renamed the Professional Football Capital of the World. Among the products of its high schools were Gene Washington, Jerry Levias, Warren Wells, Ernie Ladd, Mel and Miller Farr, Johny Fuller, Gus Holloman, Anthony Guillory, Jess Phillips, Wayne Moore, Dwight Harrison, Charles Ford, Robert Pollard, Billy Wright, Wayne McDermand, and the three men named Smith—all had represented their city in the professional ranks. By "Georgia on My Mind," sung by Allen Marks, a Charlton Pollard student, the world was reminded that behind this great man was the woman known to all the athletes and friends who attended as Mama.

Next to retire was Bubba, though not as graciously as his daddy. He reported to training camp as prepared as his body would allow. A preseason game saw him on the field for over ninety-five plays. Exhausted, he moved slowly the next day in practice. From a tower above the field two coaches watched him move, Smitty and Bum Phillips discussing the coming season. Smitty asked about his plans for Bubba, and his old friend said, "No problem." Smitty went home to his Georgia with the good news.

The very next day Bum and Bubba talked. "Bum seemed as though he was reciting rather than talking to me," says Bubba. "I had known him for years, and I could sense a change that day." The plan: Bubba was to go home and rest, and he would be placed on the reserve list; a rookie from Grambling would play, and in the third preseason game, he would take a dive, pretending he was injured, be placed on the injured reserve; then Bub would return. The Oilers would be able to protect their interests in their rookie and take advantage of Bubba's experience.

"I couldn't believe that I was being misused again," Bubba recalls, "this time by a man my father had helped for years."

He followed orders, but when Bubba returned, he had his own plan, a plan that would protect himself. His desire of being a team man was dampened by Phillips's humiliating ploy. The first chance he got, he used, and the tables were turned. He had moved to his left to follow a play, and when he felt an opposing player fall on his ankles he stayed down. It had been caught on film—he knew it—and he watched his coach as he was stretchered off the field. Bubba for the first time had cheated his sport. He had had no choice. He would not sacrifice himself for his owner—he was not a slave.

He had once lied to his mother, and it had pained him for years. Now it was his sport that had turned him into a cheat. He retired that year and hid away in Los Angeles.

Tody soon followed. Odd things had begun to happen to him. A phone call from a trusted former coach was the clincher. "Don't be surprised if you're blacklisted because of Bubba's lawsuit," he was told. He understood and retired with his brother.

Tody, Tate, and Bubba were back in their playground, Los Angeles. They began new careers in the film world, Tate working for a major studio, and Tody, who had majored in communications at USC, using his training as an actors' agent. Bubba, who had made a Powerhouse candy commercial with Georgia, felt that with a bit of luck—who knew?—he always had been an actor of sorts.

His hope-to-die partners would make a connection with him, but the phone, which had never stopped ringing when he was Mr. Football, rarely made a sound. It did one Sunday in 1977, a year he would never forget. He had his day planned, and nothing would interfere with his blueprint—A hot bath to help his still muttering knee while watching the football games on television, and add a Quaalude or two, and it would be a perfect day. The phone next to the tub rang, and he answered. It was Marguerite Simpson, O. J.'s wife, and she was requesting the pleasure of Bubba's company. "For wot?" he asked.

"Bible study, Bubba."

"Right."

"I'm serious, Bubba. It's a wonderful experience that you need right now. I'll pick you up on Wednesday morning, about 9:15."

The phone clicked off, and he lowered the receiver to its cradle and scanned the ceiling, saying, "God, save me from my friends."

Three days later stubborn Marguerite came by. She was serious about her invitation, and she would chauffeur him there. He wanted to say no, thanks, but she was determined. "What the hell," he muttered. "Just the opposite," she said.

He was reassured by the doorway to the church—it was high enough for a Smith to walk through without bending.

In one hour Bubba's casual air was transformed by rage. "Who told them?" he demanded, returning to the car. Marguerite only smiled knowingly. "What the hell are you smiling about? Did you tell them my story?"

They drove home, and she explained that it wasn't his story, it was everyone's story, and it was all in the words of the Bible. Nothing else was said until they arrived at his house. "Thank you for coming with me," she said, still smiling wonderfully as she drove away.

He stood for a long moment watching her and turned and began climbing the steps to his house. Three kids on skates sailed by, yelling at the tops of their young lungs, "Hi, Bubba." He turned to wave, warned them not to get hurt, and began searching for his keys. He had forgotten them, and he went around the back way. His dog, another of Tody's malumutes, named Torch, greeted him. Breaking into houses is not a Smith specialty, and he found himself sitting near his pool, talking to Torch. "Where could the Bible that Moses gave me be?" Torch looked at his master as if to say, "Where's the Kal-Kan, kiddo?"

"I'm serious now, Torch," he said. "I had it on that first flight to Michigan State. I remember it in the dormitory, at Wonders Hall." He drew a blank, and he rose from his seat and began walking around the pool, searching his memory.

"Marcia," he said. Torch screeched to a halt and wondered who he was talking to. "No, she's not here—she's happily married now." He walked away from his thoroughly confused friend, Torch, still trying to find his Bible.

The key to his house and another key to his life was found that day. Beginning to feel strangely relaxed, he dropped fewer 'ludes that week than in hundreds of weeks past, and a new Bible was purchased.

At Bible study the next week, sitting next to Marguerite, he was surprised at how many people had come, all kinds, sizes, shapes, and colors. He spoke to them, and instead of "What's happening, niggah?" they replied, "Good morning, brother," or even "Praise the Lord."

"You can't love someone until you love yourself," the pastor said, and he read the words of the Bible. After the lesson anyone who felt ready to "accept Jesus Christ as your personal savior" was asked to raise their hand, and the athlete, trained twenty years to control each muscle of his body, found himself out of control. His right arm shot up without his brain giving the order. In school he had rarely raised his hand, not caring about the answer to any question. Today he knew the answer. His reply was that he *was* ready. His heart was beating as it had when he was about to be married. This one marriage will last forever, he told himself.

He raced to Tody's house after his acceptance, but only Tate was home. He told her of his experience and said he would return that evening. Tate said little. "Sure, Bubba, I'll tell him." He returned that evening, and Tody and Tate were listening to *Maiden Voyage*. Their house in Baldwin Hills, Los Angeles's area for professional blacks, overlooked the city, and its lights glowed like an electric game board in the purple night. A perfect time for romance, and El Toro and his Tango were warming to its call, though Tate had told him of his brother's day, and he had replied, characteristically, "Sheeet."

The doorbell rang, and Tody repeated the word and waited for whoever it was to leave. It never stopped. He sighed deeply and allowed his wife to answer it. Bubba breezed past her—"Hello, Tate"—and made a beeline toward his frowning brother. He placed his hands on Tody's head.

"Hey man, what is it?" jumped from Tody's mouth.

"I've come to save you, Tody—really!"

Tody's expressive tongue was in his cheek. "This that John the Baptist shit!" he asked. Before Bubba could answer, Tody said, "Get out of my house, niggah! Are you crazy?" Bubba was stunned—he was on a mission and had been turned away.

After his brother had left, Tody dialed his parents' phone, as if calling the paramedics to a hit-and-run accident. Georgia answered. "How's my sweetheart?"

"I'm great, but your son Bubba has gone berserk."

"Bubba did what?" she asked.

"Mother, please sit down and listen to me. Charles Aaron Smith, your second son, the football person, has joined some cult and is in deep trouble." "Oh, my God."

Tody heard her yell the news to Smitty, and Smitty got on

the phone to tell his son they would be in Los Angeles tomorrow. Tody, relieved, walked over to his phonograph, looked at Tate, put the needle on the record and they began their second voyage.

The only way Bubba could bring Smitty and Georgia to any understanding of his new peace was to take them to the source. Georgia agreed to join him to hear the word. Tody looked at Smitty as Bubba and his mother drove off and walked into the house to find the dominoes.

The church was holding a special outing on the beach at Santa Monica. Georgia was used to more traditional settings, but whatever would help her son interested her. They walked from his car and joined the hundreds of people listening to the words of the Bible. The sound of nature provided a thrilling background to the voice of the pastor, and the message was so pure that Georgia, already a confirmed Christian, accepted the invitation to join.

"You should try it, sweetheart," Mama said to Tody at home. "The word of God would certainly help you, son!" The last time Tody had squealed on his brother, his grandmother, Georgia's mother, had given him a more memorable gift, so he felt lucky—confused, but lucky.

From the word of God to man's word, and man's law, he traveled. January 23, 1978. In the United States District Court of Florida, Middle District, Tampa Division. Charles "Bubba" Smith, plaintiff, versus the National Football League. It was a brand-new experience for the man from Nacogdoches, Texas, and he watched the parade of witnesses like an eagle.

The 1972 injury to him at Tampa Stadium had led to the filing of the two-and-a-half-million-dollar lawsuit by his attorneys, Tony Cunningham and T. Michael Foster of Tampa and Stanley "Counselor" Cohen of Baltimore, and Cunningham told a six-member all-white jury, before US District Judge John Miller, that Smith was injured by the marker pole because it was not properly removed from the path of the oncoming players as they fell out of bounds.

The first witness was Howard Cosell.

CHAPTER 9

...The Truth, So Help Me...

THEREUPON,

HOWARD COSELL,

being first duly sworn to tell the truth, the whole truth, and nothing but the truth, was deposed and testified as follows:

DIRECT EXAMINATION

BY MR. CUNNINGHAM:

> THE CLERK: State your name.
> THE WITNESS: My name is Howard Cosell.
> THE CLERK: Spell your last name for the record.
> THE WITNESS: C-o-s-e-l-l

BY MR. CUNNINGHAM:
- Q. Mr. Cosell, if I may, would you tell the Jury, although they might all know, what your occupation and profession is, sir?
- A. I'm a sports commentator employed by the American Broadcasting Companies.
- Q. Would you tell us if you would, sir, your background to arrive at that position with the American Broadcasting Company?
- A. The background is inconsistent with the point of my

ultimate arrival. I studied both journalism and law, journalism in undergraduate college, went to New York University School of Law, practiced law for ten years, and then quite by happenstance plunged into broadcasting, and by further happenstance was assigned to the field of sports.
Q. How long have you been involved in that part of your life's work, that of broadcasting involved with sports?
A. Twenty-five years.
Q. During that period of time, Mr. Cosell, have you had the opportunity to observe literally hundreds of the athletes in our country?
A. Yes, sir.

> MR. BURTON: If it please the Court, Mr. Cunningham is leading the witness. I don't think this witness needs leading at all.
> THE COURT: I think that's right, Mr. Cunningham.
> MR. CUNNINGHAM: Yes, sir, I certainly agree.

BY MR. CUNNINGHAM:
Q. Then in that regard, Mr. Cosell, did this cover all aspects of sports?
A. Yes, sir.
Q. You have had occasion to broadcast professional football games, have you not?
A. Yes, sir.
Q. Are you currently involved with a series of broadcasts on professional football, and I'm talking of *Monday Night Football*?
A. Yes, sir.
Q. You in connection with other sportscasters have that?
A. Frank Gifford and Don Meredith are my colleagues on *Monday Night Football*.
Q. Are you going to be involved in the broadcasting of the Pro Bowl tonight?
A. If I'm not, sir, you've got a scoop.
Q. And you and Mr. Meredith, I think, Mr. Gifford are also out there?
A. Yes, sir.
Q. Mr. Cosell, during the time that you have engaged in this business or profession, have you had an occasion to observe Bubba Smith, the plaintiff here?

A. Yes, sir.
Q. You had the opportunity to observe him in the 1971 Super Bowl, and prior thereto, you have told us, in his professional career, and I wonder as of that time what in your opinion were his abilities as far as his comparable abilities as being a defensive end in professional football?
A. I don't think there's any question about it. I don't think that even takes an expert witness to answer the question. Bubba Smith was the best defensive lineman in professional football in the year 1970. It's documented, all of the records of the all-star teams ... voting on Lineman of the Year, by every measuring yardstick. Bubba Smith was the best there was at what he did.
Q. Mr. Cosell, did you have an opportunity to observe Bubba during the 1971 season when, I believe, he became Lineman of the Year as you said a few moments ago?
A. Yes.
Q. In your opinion was that a good choice, based upon your observations of him being the Lineman of the Year?
A. Yes.

>THE COURT: That was for the year '71?
>MR. CUNNINGHAM: That's for the season of 1971, yes, Your Honor, and now we're talking about the playing season of '71, right, sir.

BY MR. CUNNINGHAM:
Q. Were you aware that Bubba Smith was injured in—well, first of all let me ask you this: Can you tell us what years he was All-Pro, whether he was All-Pro in '70, '71?
A. To the best of my recollection he was All-Pro both years.
Q. And would you tell the Jury what essentially that means, sir?
A. Annually it's one of the habits we have in sports of selecting the outstanding players in the many sports, and they constitute the All-Star teams in baseball, as

you people probably know, and in football we have the All-Pro teams.

The selections are made by the wire services, the U.P.I., the A.P. There are other polls taken involving sportscasters and sportswriters to determine those who merit being All-Pro. Bubba Smith to the best of my recollection was All-Pro both of those years.

Q. Were you aware Mr. Cosell, then, that he was injured in the summer of 1972 in an exhibition game here in Tampa?

A. I remember reading the wire service reports. . . .

Q. Had you personally had contact with Mr. Bubba Smith prior to that time as a professional football player, not only from observation, but had you met him personally and talked to him?

A. Yes. I had done a number of interviews with Mr. Smith, because as we went into the Super Bowl game of January of 1971, Bubba had the task of going against one of the other great linemen in football, a superb offensive end by the name of Rafael Wright, and Bubba and I used to have discourses on the problems of handling such a one as Rafael Wright, among many other conversations that I had had with Bubba during the tenure of his career.

Q. And Mr. Wright was also considered one of the very outstanding linemen, was he not, sir?

A. He was superb. In fact at the time I thought he might be too much for Bubba, but Bubba proved otherwise.

Q. Mr. Cosell, after his injury, did you have an opportunity to observe Bubba . . . on the field and at play?

A. Yes, sir.

Q. I believe that he did not play in 1972, but in 1973 and '74, did you have an opportunity to see him when he was playing with the Oakland Raiders?

A. Yes, sir.

Q. Can you tell the Jury whether or not, sir, in your opinion and based on your many years' experience and your observations, as to whether or not there was any change in Bubba Smith's abilities as you observed them?

A. Yes, sir. There was a radical change, drastic.

Q. Would you tell the Jury in what respect?

A. You weren't watching Bubba Smith. You were watching

a man grimly trying to hang on, reduced to mediocre, or something less than that when you remember his prior greatness. He was stripped of his mobilities and of his range. He could no longer accelerate quickly. By that we mean in football, get off the mark quickly . . . blocking people, and get to the passer, which is one of the chief tasks of the defensive end. He must defend the pass by rushing the passer and he must defend the run. Also, Bubba, when he was in his prime, despite his mammoth size, had great agility and great foot speed, relatively speaking. Thus he had a range that would enable him to pursue a ball carrier from one side of the field to the other, track him down. He'd get excellent angles in his pursuit. He could do all of those things when he was in his prime. He could do none of those things with anything like comparable efficiency when he was trying to play for the Oakland Raiders.

Q. Did you also have an opportunity to see him when he was at play with the Houston Oilers?
A. Yes, sir.
Q. In 1975–76?
A. Yes, sir.
Q. Can you describe to the Jury whether or not any change had occurred to bring back any of the greatness that you saw?
A. I didn't see any evidence of it. I thought he was a shell of what he had once been.
Q. Is that for the same reasons that you have just told the Jury, sir?
A. Yes, sir.
Q. Mr. Cosell, as a broadcaster and interviewer of many sports stars, are you familiar with the opportunities from business and an endorsement standpoint of a professional athlete when he becomes a star?
A. Yes, sir.
Q. I know that may seem a silly question, but how or why does a Bubba Smith—why is that a Bubba Smith, a man like this, suddenly becomes something that people want to either endorse their products or to speak for them or that sort of thing?
A. How and why does it happen?
Q. Yes, sir.
A. That's a simply phrased question, sir, but the complex-

ities of the answer are what I deal with, and of course I deliver a lecture at Yale University and at New York University. It relates to the whole of the sports syndrome in our society, the all-pervasive and massive impact of sports upon nearly all people in our society. There's a tendency in our society therefore to lionize, to heroize, athletes because of their on-field exploits, regardless of whether or not as individuals, human characters, they should be deserving of such lionization. That's how it happens, because people respond to athletes, to the athletic achievement, related to this huge place that sports has in our society, so they become among the most desirable of commercial commodities in our society.

Q. Is that a saleable commodity, Mr. Cosell? Is it something that people are willing to pay large sums of money for?

A. Immensely saleable, and yes, very large sums of money.

Q. Now, you mentioned a moment ago, despite what a person may be personally, we lionize them as far as ... their abilities or physical abilities are concerned. Howard, let me ask you this, sir, you say that you have known Bubba Smith personally when he was playing as a pro before this injury. Did you also know him afterwards?

A. Yes, sir.

Q. Did you see any change in him personally afterwards, after he was hurt in 1972?

A. Well, there are always changes in a man when his career is in decline, when he realizes he cannot be what once he was, so there would have to be changes in the human character, or certainly in the human personality, if not character. I don't see any change and have never seen any change in the basic decency of this man. I respect and frankly have a personal affection for him. But in terms of his personality, yes, there was. I could see evidence of depression and insecurity, such as would happen to anybody when his basic means of livelihood, plus all of the fame, all of the things that are attached to being prominent, to being in the public eye, vanished, and so there had to be subtle changes at least in his personality.

Q. Now, even though the public lionizes somebody and

admires somebody like Bubba Smith, what happens when suddenly he no longer is sacking the quarterback four times in a game and is sitting on the bench and is not a starter? What happens then to the public?
A. To the public? The public forgets.

On another day "Dandy Don" Meredith, or, as he said that day in court, "Jeff and Hazel's baby boy," testified. Asked, "How did you happen to meet Bubba?" he replied, "Head on."

He was asked to describe the kind of defensive lineman Bubba Smith was. He replied, "I tried to make friends with him as quickly as I could, and I tried to keep Bubba on my side . . . I'd run into him on several occasions. . . . He was nice. He would pick me up. That was nice."

Told of Bubba's ability to run the forty-yard dash in 4.6 seconds, he answered, "I think Bobby Lilly was probably the closest comparison I know. Bobby didn't run a 4.6 I'm sure, more like a five . . . . They're getting faster, aren't they?"

Meredith said, "I've gotten to know him over the years. He's one of your good ol' boys who happens to have a nice family. . . . I think he's a nice man. I can honestly say that I never saw a defensive lineman that was better than Bubba. There were days that I think Bubba could do things nobody else could do. . . . He played for the Colts, and then they had another guy out there, Big Daddy Lipscomb, before Bubba. I guess they were about the same size, but Big Daddy played when he felt like it. . . . I would say that Bubba, on Big Daddy's best days, was right there with him.

"I think that any athlete that has achieved any level of performance, and whatever reason might curtail you reaching that level again, it's very difficult for an athlete to accept. I feel that in a way the military and athletics prolong our adolescence. . . . We have tendencies to put so much [priority] on our performances. . . . Bubba became very discouraged, and I think fear of failure is one of the strongest impotences we have. . . . I think it [the injury] affected him from a psychological standpoint that he was unable to perform as he had at one time in his career. Each individual has to handle that in [his] own way."

THEREUPON,
    BILL CURRY,
being first duly sworn to tell the truth, the whole truth, and nothing but the truth, was deposed and testified as follows:

THE CLERK: State your name.
THE WITNESS: Bill Curry.
THE CLERK: Spell your last name for the record.
THE WITNESS: C-u-r-r-y.

DIRECT EXAMINATION

BY MR. CUNNINGHAM:
Q. Would you state your name, please, sir—excuse me. I know you've already given it, Mr. Curry. Mr. Curry, would you tell us what your profession or occupation is, sir?
A. Yes. I'm a football coach with the Green Bay Packers.
Q. And how long have you been in the coaching profession, Mr. Curry?
A. Two years.
Q. Do you have any specialty in the coaching field, if we can call it that?
A. Yes. I specialize in offensive line play, which of course involves the entire gamut of the game really.
Q. When we talk about an offensive line and defensive line, why is there such a differentiation, Mr. Curry?
A. Well, some obvious reason. What we're trying to do is to move the football obviously, and the defense has the reciprocal problem of stopping us. That's one differentiation. In terms of the talent required or the skills required to play one side or the other of the ball, by and large an offensive lineman is required to work more in concert with the people that he is coordinated with. The defensive lineman is required to play more by instinct. His own personal speed, strength, and agility is more important than it is for an offensive lineman. I'm not sure if that's what you're——
Q. Yes, that's what I'm talking about.
A. ——the gist of your question is. But offensive line play is predicated on doing things together. Defensive, of course, has to be coordinated, but is more based on an individual's personal skills than having to do things with other people.
Q. All right. We see things like they talk about calling a defensive line play. What does that mean?
A. Well, there are a lot of things a defensive line can try to do to an offense. A play can be a coordinated effort

by two defense linemen to try to destroy an offensive play. For instance a defensive end could charge inside with a tackle looping to the outside to compensate. That would be an example of defensive line. We don't normally call them plays. They're called stunts or games. That's a matter of terminology.

Q. However, on the offense, you of course have definite plays, do you not?

A. That's correct.

Q. Definite blocking assignment, that sort of thing?

A. Yes.

Q. If an offensive man is supposed to get a particular person, so to speak, in the defensive line or back field and move him one way or the other——

A. That's correct. You try to account for every defensive player or certainly those nearest to the point of attack to where you're trying to run the ball or throw it.

Q. Theoretically if you're operating an offensive play and you're entirely successful, the ball carrier obviously wouldn't be touched, or at least that's the idea, is that correct?

A. That's the idea.

Q. Does that usually happen?

A. That very rarely happens. Depending on who you are and who the defensive people are.

Q. All right. Let me ask you this: Do you know the plaintiff here, Bubba Smith?

A. Yes, I do.

Q. How long have you known Bubba?

A. I've known him since 1967.

Q. Now, prior to the time that you started coaching, Mr. Curry, what were you doing?

A. I was a player in the NFL.

Q. What was your position?

A. Offensive center.

Q. Who did you play for as offensive center during your professional football career?

A. I played for a lot of people. I started out with Green Bay. I played there two years. I played six years in Baltimore, one year in Houston, and one year in Los Angeles for a total of ten—ten years.

Q. You played actively for ten years as an offensive center, is that correct?

A. With the exception of one year in 1967 when I was a linebacker. I played defense.
Q. All right. You started out as a linebacker, is that correct, sir?
A. I started out playing offensive and defense in Green Bay. Actually I didn't play much of either. I was just on the team my first year. Then I played center in 1966. I was moved to linebacker in 1967 and then back to center in 1968.
Q. Now, during your—you say you've known Bubba Smith since 1967. How did you two happen to meet?
A. Well, we were teammates in Baltimore and he came there as a rookie in '67. I had been traded to Baltimore that same year so we arrived there at the same time.
Q. And what then did you—you played offensive center for the Colts in '67?
A. In '67 I played defense.
Q. Okay.
A. And then the next year I moved back to offense in '68. The only reason I was on defense was because we had a shortage of linebackers and—the defensive coaches were glad that I moved back to offense.
Q. Then you were playing on the same—excuse me if I use the wrong language and correct me if I do—you were playing on the same team defense unit? Is that what you call it?
A. That's right. We were on the same side of the ball for one year and then on the opposite side from there on.
Q. Now, did you have then an opportunity to observe Bubba both in practice and in active game playing?
A. Yes.
Q. In your opinion and based upon your experience and background, Mr. Curry, will you tell the Jury and court what kind of a ballplayer in your opinion Bubba Smith was in 1967 and thereafter until he got hurt.
A. Bubba Smith was one of the few players that I have ever seen who could be classified as a dominating force. He could literally take a game into his own hands because he required, in most instances, two blockers. We had entire defensive strategies that were simply based on the fact that he could destroy a center, which he could, or a tackle.
Q. What do you mean *destroy*—when you say that?

A. Well, I don't mean physically injure, although he could do that if he wanted to. It was impossible in my opinion—for instance, in one defensive set up that we had, he was moved over the offensive center, and the reason I'm familiar with it is because I had to work against him in practice.

Q. You mean you were the guy on the other side when you practiced against him?

A. I was the guy that he practiced on, yes, so I have an acquaintance with his skills. He was the strongest, quickest man I ever played against, and we used to joke about it. The offensive linemen on our team joked and talked about how glad we were that we were on the same team, and I'm as serious as I can be now, because there just aren't many people of that size that can move fast with that kind of strength, and you can bring anybody in here that ever played against him, and he'd tell you the same thing, that he was, for size-speed combination, I have never seen a player like Bubba Smith. I don't know if that answers your question, but he could dominate a football game.

Q. When you speak of two blockers, what are you talking about, why, and tell, if you would, tell us why that's important?

A. Well, obviously again, we have eleven people, and the defense has eleven people, and one of our people is going to have to have the ball. So we don't have a blocker for every defender. We would like to be able to take care of everybody, ideally, with one on one situations. If there's a defensive player that requires two blockers, then obviously that leaves somebody else unblocked and creates real problems for the offense. So if there's a dominating player, a player like Bubba—or another example would have been Bob Lilly, people like that—then it restricts your offense and creates serious problems for you and you have to change your game play, and you have to change your strategy. You have to change your entire approach because of a player like that. It restricts what you can do. Therefore the defense is able to predict more accurately what you're likely to do, and they can all close in on you, and that's why a person like that becomes a number-1 draft choice, or plays in the Pro Bowl, or all the things that goes along with being a great player.

Q. Have you seen on occasion when despite the fact that there were two blockers on Bubba Smith, that he has still got involved in a play, and I mean by that, got some hand on either the ball carrier or the quarterback or somebody that had the ball?

A. Yes, there were those times. Usually when you double-team a man, you expect that to hold up, and it should, and we worked very hard. Offense in general works very hard to make sure that that doesn't happen, but there were times when he beat the double-team.

Q. In your opinion, Mr. Curry, in a one-on-one situation, did you ever observe any football player that in your opinion could successfully block Bubba Smith prior to his injury?

A. There were other good players on offense who had some success, but for an entire game I never saw anybody handle him consistently, no.

Q. Are you familiar with the time when Bubba Smith was injured here in Tampa at the Tampa Stadium?

A. Yes. I was there.

Q. At that time what were you playing, what position?

A. I was an offensive center. I was not actually in the game. I was on the sidelines when the injury occurred. . . .

Q. Mr. Curry, have you seen that play before on movie film?

A. Yes. . . .

Q. Now, let me ask you this question: Mr. Curry, in looking at this, can you . . . identify the relative players and their position at that moment? If you can. . . .

A. Yes. Well, what the play is is a pass by the Steelers, as you can see. Rick Volk intercepted the ball. Baltimore was rushing the passer, and when [Smith] saw an interception, he began to peel back this way to try to block. Now he becomes an offensive player. What he's trying to do is block for the ball carrier, and when he throws his body, of course, he flies out of bounds, and that's what he's trying to do.

Q. Is this what he's supposed to be doing as a ballplayer from his position?

A. Yes. Something that offensive people work very hard on is to prevent long runbacks on interceptions. Defensive people try to stress the need, once your defensive back has intercepted the ball, or linebacker, for the defensive linemen to now become a blocker and to turn back and help, and that's what's happening here. If you're alert, and if you're in the game as a defensive player, now you'll turn back and try to find somebody, one of the others, the opposing team's players, and try to block him so that you can advance the ball as far as possible.

Q. Where's Bubba in that picture, coach?

A. I believe this is Bubba here, if I'm not mistaken. It's kind of hard to be sure.

Q. All right. Is that Rick Volk who looks like he's coming out to shake his hands there at the moment or something?

A. Yes. He's just eluding one guy.

Q. That's the player on the ground?

A. Yes.

Q. And in your opinion as coach, is Bubba playing properly, as you see this sequence, and is he doing what he's supposed to be doing as a professional football player and as a defensive end?

A. Absolutely. One of the marks of a good defensive team, on an interception they'll all rally around the ball carrier and again try to get a block rather than to just stand there and watch him.

Q. Coach, based on your playing experience and your coaching, when a player is going to come to the sidelines, or is coming like this, like Bubba is here, to block for the ball carrier, is it both permissible and proper play to keep running—in other words, to go out of bounds.

A. There's no way to avoid it. If you're running as fast as you can and the field of play includes every inch from sideline to sideline literally, you don't slow up as you approach the sideline or somebody will run right by you. You'll miss the block or the tackle or whatever you're trying to do. So, very often you'll come out of this, off this playing field through the sideline area just gangbusters, just as fast as you can go. It happens all the time, and you're instructed as a player, if anybody, your teammate or an opposing team player, comes out of bounds like that, to try to catch him and to break his speed so that he won't injure himself.

Q. In other words all ballplayers are taught that if you're on the sidelines?

A. Yeah. It's just something you try to do. You have to protect yourself but also your teammate or the other player, because the point is, to answer your question, coming off the sideline, you're coming full speed. . . .

Q. During the time, coach, that you saw Bubba coming towards that, were you watching him, watching that play?

A. I was watching the whole play. As a lineman, the reason I hesitated when you asked me if I saw Rick Volk catch the ball, I probably didn't. I was watching the line play. I would study the pass rush of our people and the protection of the Steelers, and then when you hear a roar, then you start to look around, but you're still focusing on the linemen, and I do remember Bubba coming this way and throwing his body and going into the crowd. That's what I remember.

Q. All right, sir. Now, at the time that you remember that, could you in fact—did you have in your visual field the standard or the pole that we're talking about there in the picture?

A. Well, as I said earlier, I had it in my field of vision, but I was not standing there concentrating on the pole. I can't say that I was, but that was in my field of vision, and as I said, all I remember was seeing him go into the area where the pole was with the official there. . . .

Q. And as you were looking at it, until the time that Bubba went into that area, that you saw him disappear, as far as you were able to observe, was that pole ever removed or taken back from the field of play?

A. It was not.

REDIRECT EXAMINATION

BY MR. CUNNINGHAM:

Q. Coach, let me ask you one other thing: As a player, and your experience as a player and as a coach, when you're heading towards the sidelines in a play, can you tell this Jury whether or not you rely upon the fact that

if there's a standard there or a pole or something like
that, that the official holding that, that he's going to
get out of your way?
A. That's his job. Any official on the field or more importantly on the sideline is supposed to get out of your way. Sometimes they do and sometimes they don't.
Q. Do you as a player or did you as a player rely upon the fact that they would get out of the way?
A. Yes.

The damaging testimony, that of George Wilson, former coach of the Washington Redskins, the Detroit Lions, and the Miami Dolphins, introduced the name of Franco Harris to the trial. His so-called expert testimony suggested that, on film, Bubba had hit Franco, or vice versa, which had led to the injury. Franco Harris failed to remember, before seeing the film. The trial ended in frustration—a hung jury.

He watched them all leave, and he waved a one-finger goodnight to his lawyers, who looked bewildered. Stanley, who had been looking extremely tired walked over to him, and they shook hands. Bubba's left hand rested over their clasped hands. "Hang in, Cuddy Cuddy," Stanley said. "I understand, good pardner, I do understand." He smiled, and Stanley left the courtroom.

A bailiff, who a week before had asked for Bubba's autograph, was the only person left in the courtroom besides Bubba. The bailiff looked, shifted his weight from one foot to the other, then looked at his watch, twice. Smith received the message loud and clear, glanced at the American flag that stood to the right, behind the empty judge's seat, shook his head, and rose from his seat. He loosened the knot of his silken tie, and unbuttoned his collar, and walked out slowly. His footsteps on the marble floor echoed.

He lit a cigarette, thinking he should stop. His trial was over; the enemy had won. But he had told the truth, and there would be another trial in a higher court someday. And this one could be a warning of sorts to young athletes, those who had accepted his torch, kids, as he was once, with wide eyes who thought only of having fun and team play.

Citizen Smith checked his watch and looked to both his left and right. His left hand began patting his pants leg in a staccato rhythm. He began humming "Reasons," the Earth, Wind and Fire classic, as if waiting for someone. It was dark now, and Tampa, like so many cities, had closed early. Bubba strode down the courthouse steps and walked to his hotel.

He was on the phone to Los Angeles and Tody. Tody said, "Whatever you do, come home, now." It was a direct order, and Bubba never questioned it. He packed and booked to the Tampa airport.

He waited for his 11:45 flight, and the pain began to ease. He glanced to his right, and a television set was on. It was the news announcing, "Details of the Bubba Smith trial next." A citizen of Tampa, half the size of Bubba and without a trace of color, who was watching the tube with him, said, "Those chickenshit. . . . " He was referring to the words on the screen: NFL WINS. Bubba leaned over to the man and said, "You don't know how right you are."

The boarding sign was up, and Bubba was the first passenger on board.

A smooth flight, it landed in Los Angeles on schedule, and a cab sped him to Tody's house. The door was wide open, as it always is, and he dropped his suitcases in the foyer and walked, like a man twice his age, up the stairs.

Hearing the footsteps, Tody came out of the bedroom, and the brothers met at the top step. "Let that shit go, Bub. Those people will drive you crazy." He could see the deep pain in his brother, and he put his arm around his brother's neck. They sat, as they had so many years ago, at the top of the stairs, both staring down at the living room below.

"Why, man?" Bubba began. "Why did they lie? I never tried to hurt anybody in my life! Why would they?"

"A whole bunch of folks have tried and will continue to try to hurt us, but it still hasn't happened." The Tody smile enveloped his face.

And the tears fell from both men, happy to have someone to cry with.

But that which ye have already hold fast till I come.
And he that overcometh, and keepeth my works unto the end, to him will I give power over the nations. . . . I am the root and the offspring of David, and the bright and morning star.

—The Revelation of St. John the Divine 2:25–26; 22:16

AFTERWORD

Stanley "Counselor" Cohen passed away in the spring of 1982, a victim of leukemia. Bubba was at his bedside.

Bubba and his brother Tody are members of Crenshaw Christian Center. They learn from and worship with their pastor, Frederick K. Price.

Smitty and Georgia dance to "Music, Maestro, Please" every chance they get. Yes, they do!

About Hal DeWindt

Born and raised in Harlem, New York. Actor and model (*Ebony* magazine Model of the Year, 1957–61). Production stage manager: New York Shakespeare Festival. Stage manager: John F. Kennedy and Lyndon B. Johnson White House Salutes. Director of training: Negro Ensemble Company. Production manager: New York Philharmonic. Assistant vice-president: Paramount Studios. Director of development: Universal Studios (New Ventures). Professor: Black Theatre, Cal State Northridge. Author of two films: *The Black Prince* and "Us Versus Nobody." Associate producer: *The Angel Levine* (Harry Belafonte); *The Landlord* (Norman Jewison); *They Call Me Mr. Tibbs* (Sidney Poitier); *A Hero Ain't Nothin' But a Sandwich* (Robert Radnitz). Director of his own theatre workshop in Los Angeles. And last, but far from least, Bubba Smith's bodyguard.